M000266294

Victoriously Dancing Throug...

Written with eloquence and clarity, Victoriously Dancing Through Life is a powerful testimony of Jacquie's faith in, reliance on, and glorification of God. Thrown into the lion's den like Daniel, it is a story of courage. God's revelation of His power gave Jacquie spiritual authority that enabled her to tell about Jesus Christ in the face of her adversity. Instead of complaining and regressing into self-pity, Jacquie writes her story in a candid manner. It is a story of God turning tragedy into victory. It is a story of God doing immeasurably more than all we ask or imagine. Indeed, all things work together for good to those who love God. As a believer, I commend this book with great joy and love.

Ambassador James L. Kateka
Judge of the International Tribunal for the Law of the Sea
Hamburg, Germany

If you are expecting a novel that focuses only on breast cancer prepare to be surprised. This book offers several pillars of support Jacquie Vick discovered that inspired her dance through a gut-wrenching diagnosis. Victoriously Dancing Through Life is a must-read for you, a family member, or a friend experiencing a similar challenge.

Cheryl Burton, certified self-leadership coach,
Christian counselor, author

As a breast cancer survivor, this book confirms the sentiments of my physicians and Godmother—"strong mental and spiritual beliefs will strengthen your walk with God and increase your capacity to persevere during treatment." Victoriously Dancing Through Life would have helped me navigate the many challenges and obstacles we face. Whatever your "it" is, this faith book will greatly assist you in finding victory! I strongly urge you to read it and let the joy and comfort of God's Word fill your soul.

L. Wynette Murphy, MD, FACOG

A Spiritual Guide to Overcome...Breast Cancer was My "It"

Victoriously Dancing Through Life, Orchestrated by God

Jacquie Vick

Victoriously Dancing Through Life Orchestrated by God

A Spiritual Guide to Overcome…Breast Cancer was My "It"

Disclaimer

The information found in this book is not intended to be a substitute for professional medical advice, diagnosis, or treatment. Always seek the advice of your physician with any questions you may have regarding a medical condition. Never disregard professional medical advice or delay in seeking it because of something you have read in this book. If you think you may have a medical emergency, call your doctor, go to the emergency room of your local hospital, or call 911 immediately.

All Scripture quotations, unless otherwise stated, are taken from The Holy Bible, New King James Version and the New International Version found on BibleHub.com.

Credits

Editor: Kim Sadler

Sadler Communications & Consulting Group, LLC.

Graphic Design: Elaine Young

Hopscotch Communications

Cover Illustrator: Ciara Hudson

DEDICATION

To my Lord and Savior Jesus Christ

I give all the glory to my Lord and Savior, Jesus Christ,
for my dance, His presence in my life, and the angels
He has encamped around me...I was
(and still am) in His safety.

To my mom, Mini Vick, who stayed on her knees in prayer,
giving thanks to our Father for His goodness. She, like many of
us, grew spiritually as we witnessed God's faithfulness!

~ It Takes a Village ~

Wait, there's much more...God is AWESOME!

I invite you to reference the Acknowledgements section
of this book to see the many people God placed along
the path of my dance.

CONTENTS

CONTENTS
conitnued

FOREWORD

If you were handed a bunch of lemons, what would you do? Many people would say make lemonade, which is exactly what Jacquie decided to do as she faced one of the most challenging times in her life. I am not surprised by Jacquie's response to difficult challenges. As a colleague, I observed her passion, tenacity, and can-do attitude as president of the National Black MBA Association-Saint Louis Chapter and as president of Primary Conversations Toastmasters Club in St. Louis, MO. Through our friendship, I soon realized that this is how she approaches everything in life, even her encounter with breast cancer.

Victoriously Dancing Through Life, Orchestrated by God embodies Jacquie's faith and trust in our Heavenly Father and His divine plan and purpose in her life. I say our Father because she is not only a professional colleague and friend but, more importantly, my sister in Christ! It is her relationship with Christ that enabled her to cry out, "Though He slay me, yet will I trust Him" (Job 13:15). Jacquie decided to trust Him, and her victorious attitude has inspired me to trust our Heavenly Father even more.

Whenever we are faced with life challenges, trusting God is the key. We must trust and know that all things work together for good to those who love God and are called according to

His purpose (Romans 8:28). God had a purpose, and I am so glad Jacquie was able to recognize it. She intends to reveal the power of God in her life and how His Word can heal physically, spiritually, and emotionally.

This book will take you on the emotional highs and lows of Jacquie's journey. Yet, it will awaken your spirit and make you realize that you too "can do all things through Christ who gives you the strength!" (Philippians 4:13). Your personal trial may be different than Jacquie's, but one thing is for certain: God is able! He is able to keep you in perfect peace and strengthen you so that you too can dance victoriously in the midst of the storm.

Rev. Dr. Jeffrey A. Williams
Senior Pastor, New Christian Fellowship Church
Fairview Heights, IL

PREFACE

He Knows My Name

Eye has not seen, nor ear heard,
Nor have entered into the heart of man
The things which God has prepared for
those who love Him.
~ 1 Corinthians 2:9 ~

I begin my book with a title inspired by Tasha Cobbs Leonard's song featuring Jimi Cravity, "You Know My Name." The song reminds me that God knows my name. He knows me, and nothing that happens to me is a surprise to Him. Everything has a purpose, and He will use it for His glory. Approximately 20 years ago, I started writing a fiction novel and stopped after about eight chapters. According to my longtime friend Gilda, it was a page-turner! As I completed a chapter, I would send it to her for feedback. To this day, she will often ask, "When are you going to finish that book?" Initially, I couldn't discern precisely why I had stopped. Years later, I realized I wanted to write a book that would add value to and impact the reader's life. Fast forward, life's circumstances have allowed me to accomplish this as co-author of this book with God. God knew this day would come. He prepared me and worked it out for my good and His purpose. He is truly "the author and finisher of my life."

My dance, through blinding rains of tears and triumphant shouts of joy, has already impacted others. Praise God! There is joy in knowing that God knows me. God knows my heart, the number of hairs on my head, and the number of days I will be on this side of Heaven! There is joy in knowing that He has already perfected everything that pertains to me. The path God has for me has been made clear! Thank you, Father, in the name of Jesus.

Confession of Faith

From the start of my dance with cancer, God was clear, "...Fear not, for I am with you; Be not dismayed, for I am your God, I will strengthen you, Yes, I will help you, I will uphold you with My righteous right hand" (Isaiah 41:10).

Isaiah 41:10, one of my favorite scriptures, was my go-to scripture whenever I was fearful. I give all the glory to my Lord and Savior, Jesus Christ, for holding me and guiding me in this dance. Each day I felt His presence in my life and the angels He had encamped around me. I was, and still am, in His safety. I understand that this was my process, and I thank God for it because it drew me closer to Him!

Victoriously Dancing Through Life, Orchestrated by God is an inspirational account of my spiritual dance through the life-threatening diagnosis of cancer and God's victory in my healing. As in a dance, I had to bend, stretch, turn, rise, and glide through a diagnosis that helped me learn about myself and my relationship with God. Some would see this dance as dark moments where I had to dart through a series of storms, but I embraced the dance because of my relationship with God. I did not operate in my strength. I depended on God's power to lead and carry me victoriously through the process. I knew I had no control over the outcome, so I relaxed in my faith and His arms, knowing He was with me. I rejoiced and sang songs of praise in the midst of the unknown. I held on to God's righteous right hand and allowed His Spirit to carry me through this dance. Together we danced. He led, and I followed!

My willingness to let God lead in this dance did not start with my diagnosis. It began when I accepted Jesus Christ as my Lord and Savior. In 2013, I was strengthened when I joined a Bible study group. I learned the importance and benefits of spending daily intentional and purposeful time reading God's Holy Word. As a result, I experienced spiritual growth. Reading God's Word allowed it to "dwell in [me] richly" (Colossians 3:16), rejoicing and praying and giving thanks. This spiritual discipline prepared me for the events of 2016 when I received the diagnosis of cancer.

As a part of my daily prayers, I say the "Confession of Faith." It is a participatory reading recited by my Bible study group at the start of each session. In the beginning, while I did not fully grasp the magnitude of its content, I participated in the corporate reading. It had become a bedrock in my spiritual dance to recovery and healing. The more I read the "Confession of Faith," the more the Holy Spirit reveals its meaning to me—and the more I understand the power and authority I possess.

~

"Heavenly Father, I thank you because I am a believer who is in covenant with you through Jesus Christ. I have authority over demonic activity. No weapon formed against me shall prosper in any way. I plead the blood of Jesus over my life, my family, and all that belongs to me. I take authority over every demonic force that comes against me in the name of Jesus. Because I am the righteousness of God, in my pathway, there is light and no darkness. I have been translated out of the kingdom of darkness and into the light of your dear son, Jesus. Because I am in a relationship with Him, I am seated with Him in Heavenly places far above every demonic spirit and principality. I exercise my authority by speaking the Word of God by faith. I am victorious and more than a conqueror through Christ Jesus, who dwells in me. Greater is He that is in me than he that is in the world. I cancel every demonic assignment and bind every demon that comes against me. I loose the anointing of God to remove every burden and destroy every yoke in my life. I am no longer subject to the curse because I am submitted to the Word of God. In Jesus' name, I pray [and give thanks]. Amen. Amen. Amen."

~

Scripture tells us that we all will face trials and tribulations in life. No matter what the challenges might be, those of us who are called by His name will never have to go through them alone. God is with us. Believe in, lean on, and trust in Him.

If you do not know the Lord, He knows you!
"Psalm 139 provides us with tremendous insight into the Father's perfect knowledge of who we are and His abundant love for us.

XIII

God made us. God knows our weaknesses. God knows our sinful desires. None of our transgressions are hidden from Him. He knows our innermost hurts, fears, and frustrations..."[1] Yet, despite our faults, God longs to have a personal relationship with us. We have to accept His invitation. Invite Him into our lives. He is patiently waiting!

In reading this book, I hope you will see and feel God's presence guiding and leading me through the bends and turns of my dance. I also hope you will invite Jesus to be a daily part of your life so when you experience trials, you will be more than ready to face them armed with God's truth. "...He is the One who goes before you. He will be with you; He will not leave you nor forsake you..." (Deuteronomy 31:8). It is my prayer that Victoriously Dancing Through Life, Orchestrated by God will inspire you to know the Father through Christ Jesus, our Lord and Savior. I pray that you will dig deeper into the biblical stories shared in this book. If you are not a part of a church, I pray that God will lead you to a Bible-teaching church so that you may learn and grow in God's Word. "...let us consider one another in order to stir up love and good works, not forsaking the assembling of ourselves together..." (Hebrews 10:24-25). More importantly, I pray that you will allow the Holy Spirit to guide and direct you. I share this with you because it is in God's Word that you find love, peace, comfort, and joy through Jesus! Amen!

INTRODUCTION

Blessing and Burden

"...Blessed are those who hear the word of God and keep it!"
~ Luke 11:28 ~

If you are reading these words, you need a blessing. God has directed you to hope, strength, and comfort during your trials and tribulations. Victoriously Dancing Through Life, Orchestrated by God chronicles my dance, faith walk, and trust in God through the most challenging time in my life. This book is about the assurance of knowing I am not alone. Therefore, I can victoriously face any trial in life. Jesus Christ walks with me and gives me the strength to not just walk but to dance with Him as I face life challenges. And guess what, He is with you too!

In February 2016, without preparation, I was thrown into a storm. I joined a club that I never aspired to join, but suddenly, my name appeared on the roster. As a soldier for the Lord, unbeknownst to me, He prepared me for this storm. God will use my situation for His glory. The Bible tells us we will all experience trials and tribulations in this life, so we have a choice. We can go it alone and be miserable and afraid, or we can take God's righteous right hand and let His Spirit guide us and carry us through the dance. When we trust God, we will have peace and joy that surpasses understanding during the process. In Him, we have the comfort of knowing He is with us and will never leave us. The only way to experience His joy and peace is to trust and believe in Him with your heart, mind, and soul.

Some years ago, in a conversation with my mom, she asked me, "Would you recognize God's voice if He spoke to you?" I remember giving an uncertain response. Truthfully, I did not know if I would recognize His voice. After all, what does God's voice sound like? How would I know if He were speaking to me? I felt bad when I realized I could not respond confidently. I could feel my shoulders drop and sadness come over me. I knew I was a believer and had accepted Jesus Christ as my Lord and Savior, but outside of the church, I did not spend time with Him by reading and meditating on His Word. Then one day....

I'm not sure when or even where I got the information, so let's just say God put it in my hands. I read an article by Charles Stanley titled "How God Gets Our Attention" in the March 2004 issue of In Touch Ministries. The article stated, "God speaks to us through scripture, circumstances, prayer, and other people; but we are helpless to hear God apart from the Holy Spirit who enables us to hear what God is saying."[1] As I read the article, I had an "aha moment" – a light bulb came on. As a result, my time in God's Word became much more intentional, and I read with the expectation that God was speaking to me through scripture. I would get the same feeling when my pastor, Bishop Jones, delivered God's Word in a sermon — I often felt the message was just for me. As I paid closer attention and took copious notes, I realized I was becoming spiritually alert and open to receiving God's Word.

Friday, March 4, 2016, began as a regular, ordinary day. I took my routine long hot shower in preparation for my first day of chemotherapy treatments. This day, however, proved to be no ordinary day. It was the day that my spirit was in alignment with God's will. I was spiritually alert. Surprisingly I was relaxed. My mind was blank—so I thought. As I mentally prepared for the day ahead of me, I thanked God for waking me up, covering me, and preparing me for round one of six chemotherapy treatments. Not knowing what to expect, I dismissed everything I heard and read about chemo's side effects. Instead, I accepted that this was my process. I knew I was not on this journey alone — God was by my side, communicating with me constantly through His Word, daily readings, meditations, and fellow believers. Then, while still standing in the shower, I heard God's voice. It was clear, so clear, that I stepped out of the shower, found a piece of paper and a pen to write down what He said to me. Now, in all honesty, there was no loud, robust voice, and I don't recall Him saying, Jacquie,

I want you to write a book. My mind, however, was flooded with the title of this book, a few chapter titles, and the format. I sat on the side of the detached tub, just below the skylight. I felt joyful and overwhelmed. I knew I had heard the voice of God through His Spirit because of the peace I experienced! I then dressed and grabbed my bag of goodies that included reading material, logic problems, and some snacks. My mom and my Aunt Catherine had come to accompany me to the hospital. I began my journey, not giving much thought to what had happened. I really did not know what to think, so I focused on getting to the hospital and what was to come.

Scripture tells us that God loves to bless obedience, but I was far from being obedient with the task given to me. I told myself I had plenty of time. After all, God did not want me to write this book until my treatments were completed. I began jotting down notes here and there and did nothing more with them. I convinced myself I would wait until completing my treatments in September and after I decided about reconstructive surgery. As a result of my lack of urgency to write, I became restless — not a day went by that I did not think about writing this book.

On April 3, 2018, just over one and a half years after my treatments, I shared my "God encounter" with Curtis, my brother in Christ. "You have to write the book," he said emphatically. "If you want," he further said, "I will be your accountability partner." He said, "God has given you an assignment, and you must be obedient." So, we devised an accountability plan for the next steps and action items. After a while, despite Curtis' best efforts to keep me on task, I experienced writer's block and was not always motivated to write. Quite frankly, I was often discouraged and disappointed with myself. After all, I am a writer, and this should not happen. Moreover, this is my story. How difficult could it be to write my story? Well, it wasn't easy, and I found it to be more challenging than I thought. Where should I start? What should I share? How will it be shared? What would be too much information or not enough information? These were just a few questions I had.

On Monday, November 19, 2018, I sat at my L-shaped glass office desk, picked up The Word for You Today daily devotional, and began reading "Dare to Dream." In the body of this writing, the author asked, "How can you tell if your vision is from God?" The answer, "It will bless you and benefit others."[2] This lit a fire in me! At that moment, I remembered my desire to write a book that would be impactful to others! God was allowing me to use my experience for His Glory. Victoriously Dancing Through Life, Orchestrated by God is not of my doing; it is of God! "That which is born of the flesh is flesh; And that which is born of the Spirit is Spirit" (John 3:6). From that day forward, my life changed for the better because of my relationship with Christ! Revelation 12:11 tells us, "And they overcame him by the blood of the Lamb and by the words of their testimony." This book is not for me; it's for you. With this book, I glorify and honor the Father and receive His blessings through my testimony! I started thinking that this book had to be perfect and correct, but I realized it had to be authentic. I simply had to tell my story.

Moment of Clarity
It's easy to think this book is only for someone diagnosed with cancer, but this is so not true. This book is for anyone who has had to trust and lean on God, irrespective of what they have faced or will face in life. Cancer was my experience. The loss of a child might be your experience. Diagnosis with another disease might be your experience. No matter what you might go through, it is my hope and prayer that through my testimony, you will realize that our Father is with you and will help you through your "it." The "it" of your trial or tribulation can only be successful if you surrender and let Him guide you through your dance. The "it" may or may not be easy, but your ability to go through "it" is by God's grace and mercy. He has given us instructions. As Kim, the leader of my Bible study group often says, "The Bible is your policy and procedure!"

Reflection

This is a moment for you to reflect on your "God encounter." Journal the experience: Where were you? What were you doing? How did you feel? Who did you tell? What were you tasked with doing? Did you follow through?

Reflection Questions for Discussion

1. Do you believe trials and tribulations are designed to get your attention? Grow you spiritually? Build your faith and trust in God? (Reference: Romans 12:12; 1 Corinthians 10:13; James 1:2-8, 12)

2. When you encounter life's challenges, do you seek God's counsel first? If not, what prevents you from turning to God first? (Reference: Matthew 6:33)

3. On the road to Damascus, Paul had a "God encounter." What was your "Damascus moment?" Did you recognize the Holy Spirit speaking to you? If so, did you consider your task to be a blessing or a burden? Why? Why not? Have you seen the fruits of your labor? Who has your obedience to God blessed? How have you been blessed? (Reference: Acts 9)

4. What's your moment of clarity?

_____

_____

_____

_____

_____

_____

_____

_____

_____

_____

_____

_____

_____

_____

_____

_____

_____

_____

Section One
Bending My Ear to Hear God (*Listening*)

So then faith comes by hearing, and hearing by the Word of God.
~ Romans 10:17 ~

"In the Old Testament God marked His priests by putting blood on their right ear lobe, their right thumb, and the big toe of their right foot. That meant they were called to honor God in their hearing, their skills, and their daily walk. You can't just do your own thing; you're called to walk according to God's Word."[1]

"Everything that we need to know in regard to salvation—what it is, why we need it, how we can receive it—can be found in God's Word. God blesses us when we hear His promises and respond in faith to them."[2]

CHAPTER 1

The Elephant in the Room

*But He was wounded for our transgressions, He was bruised for
our iniquities; the chastisement for our peace was upon Him,
And by His stripes, we are healed.*
~ Isaiah 53:5 ~

Don't be afraid... Just have faith, and [you] will be healed.
~ Luke 8:50 ~

In February 2016, I became aware of my mortality. Like so many,
I took waking up every morning and going about my busy day
for granted. Perhaps this passage into reality comes with time,
age, knowledge, and wisdom. However it comes to be, I was
acutely aware of it when the doctor said, "The test results show
that you have stage three triple-negative breast cancer." I could
feel my heart sink. My invisible, silent tears were there, but my
faith was not shaken. That's the elephant in the room. But let's
back up. How did this come about?

In late July or early August of 2015, I felt two small lumps, one
under my left armpit and the other on the left side of my left
breast. I did not ignore the lumps but thought I would monitor
them to see if they grew, moved, or dissolved. I took this
approach because when I was in my teens, I discovered a lump.
My doctor monitored it to see if it would grow, move, or dissolve.
It eventually went away. I have learned that this noncancerous
breast tumor called fibroadenoma is common in young women.
Fibroadenoma is a solid, noncancerous breast lump. In my late
30s or early 40s, I had a mammogram. The mammogram results

showed calcium deposits which required a biopsy. This minor surgical procedure left a welted scar on my left breast. The biopsy result was negative. This time, I played doctor and decided to keep a watchful eye on the lumps based on those previous events. Then one morning, I checked the lumps, and to my surprise and fright, both were HUGE. Not thinking the worst but recognizing this needed immediate attention, I quickly scheduled my yearly well woman's visit. During the examination, my doctor shared my concern and immediately scheduled a mammogram.

Following the mammogram, the mammographer escorted me to the waiting room and asked me to wait while the radiologist viewed the images. She soon returned with an expression of alarm on her face. She shared that the radiologist wanted me to have an ultrasound because of the size of the masses. Everyone who saw me that day tried to remain as calm as possible, but they were visibly concerned. I remember the look on the face of a second mammographer entering the room following the ultrasound – she had a sorrowful, despairing look on her face – a look that said what she just learned about me was a death sentence. I remember saying to her, "Don't worry about me. I will be okay."

My gynecologist saw the test results and immediately recommended I see a breast surgeon. His assistant contacted me with the name and phone number of the recommended surgeon. For some strange reason, I felt a sense of shame. I felt as if there was some stigma associated with having to make the call. Nonetheless, I thanked the assistant for the information. Shortly thereafter, I called to schedule the appointment for the following week. The breast surgeon had numerous questions at the initial meeting. "When did you notice the lumps?" he asked. "Around August 2015," I responded. "Why did you wait?" he further asked. I responded by saying, "I monitored the lumps to see if they grew, moved, or went away." He inquired further. "Is there a history of breast cancer in your family?" he asked, trying to dig deeper. "Maternally, a first cousin was diagnosed with breast cancer about 15 years ago. Paternally, my dad's sisters were diagnosed with breast cancer in their 70s," I said. "Are you feeling any discomfort or pain?" he asked with urgency. "No," I answered with concern.

The questioning continued, which, unintentionally, made me feel shameful and embarrassed. Silently, I started to question my decision to wait. After the series of questions, I was asked to lie back on the elongated table with my left arm above my head. The feel and size of the lumps were alarming. The doctor scheduled an in-office needle biopsy for the lump in the left breast and the lump under the left arm. Two weeks later, before going to work, I arrived at the office for the procedure that took all of 20 minutes. I dressed and headed to work. I left the doctor's office feeling hopeful and prayerful that all was well with me and not giving much thought to the procedure I had had. I certainly never thought the diagnosis would be breast cancer. After all, I was not a smoker. However, my worst fears were realized during my third visit with the surgeon.

Moment of Clarity

The doctor and nurses had seen cases like mine before, and based on experience, knew the consequences could be fatal. The concerned faces said it all, but Jeremiah 1:8 says, "Do not be

5

afraid of their faces, For I am with you to deliver you, says the Lord." As a believer, I had to be careful of others' energy and not take my focus off God, which is exactly what the enemy wanted. The enemy wanted me to focus on my issue and not on my God and His grace. Scripture says, "Cast all your care on Him [your refuge] because He cares for you" (1 Peter 5:7). He will direct your path!

Reflection

This is a moment for you to reflect on your "elephant in the room." Journal the experience: Where were you? How did you respond? How did you feel? Who did you tell? Did you seek additional information, or did you just accept the situation?

_____

_____

_____

_____

_____

_____

_____

_____

_____

_____

_____

_____

_____

_____

_____

_____

CHAPTER 1 ~ The Elephant in the Room

Reflection Questions for Discussion

1. When problems arise, do you tend to ignore them out of fear? Are you hoping the problem(s) will go away? Does that help or hinder resolution?

2. How do you face life's problems/challenges? Do you face them head on? Do you seek counsel from family, friends, clergy? Do you pray and ask God in the name of Jesus by His Spirit to guide you?

3. Are you influenced by the responses and actions of others? Do you allow past events to dictate your decision-making process?

4. What's your moment of clarity?

_____

_____

_____

_____

_____

_____

_____

_____

_____

_____

_____

_____

_____

_____

_____

_____

_____

_____

_____

CHAPTER 1 ~ The Elephant in the Room

_____

_____

_____

_____

_____

_____

_____

_____

_____

_____

_____

_____

_____

_____

_____

_____

_____

_____

_____

_____

_____

_____

_____

_____

_____

_____

_____

_____

_____

_____

_____

_____

CHAPTER 2

※

Joy in My Dance

*Therefore, humble yourselves under the mighty hand of God,
that He may exalt you in due time, casting all your care upon
Him, for He cares for you. Be sober, be vigilant; because your
adversary the devil walks about like a roaring lion, seeking whom
he may devour. Resist him, steadfast in the faith, knowing that the
same sufferings are experienced by your brotherhood in the world.
But may the God of all grace, who called us to His eternal glory
by Christ Jesus, after you have suffered a while, perfect, establish,
strengthen, and settle you.*
~ 1 Peter 5:6-10 ~

With my sanctified imagination, I can only imagine how it was
when the woman with the issue of blood traveled to see Jesus.
It was hot from the sun's rays, no shade, and the air was dusty
from the multitude of people on the road. Not expecting to
speak to Jesus, the woman made up her mind that she would
be healed if she could just touch the hem of his garment. And
after doing so, she was healed. Jesus said to her, "Daughter, be of
good cheer, your faith has made you well" (Luke 8:48). Unlike
the day the woman touched the hem of Jesus' garment, it was
a cold winter's day with clear skies on February 18, the day of
my doctor's appointment. Watching the time, I finished my work
and pushed back my chair from the desk. I stood up, grabbed my
brown tweed coat and red Delta Sigma Theta scarf, and headed
to the employee's parking lot. It was 30 minutes before my third
appointment with the breast surgeon. When I arrived, I took
a deep breath and said a quick prayer before reaching for the
metal door handle to enter the medical building. Once inside the
sterile environment, I made my way to the elevator. I tried to be
nonchalant but found it difficult to focus on any one thing. Even
as I entered the office, checked in, and sat in the waiting area, I
was moving in automatic mode. "Ms. Vick," I heard someone say.
I looked up and made eye contact with the attending nurse. "The

doctor will see you now." I followed the nurse down the hall to a familiar room. "Let me get your vitals, and then the doctor will come in," she said. "Okay," I responded. Before the nurse left the room, I tried to read her face, but nothing about her demeanor gave any indication of the test results.

"Tap, tap." The doctor entered. His standard greeting was pleasant, and then he revealed the results of the test. I sat across from him with a blank stare, like a deer in headlights. He shared that the biopsy results showed I had triple-negative breast cancer, and the masses ranged from 2.5 to 3.5cm in diameter. As he began to talk about the recommended steps for treatment, chemotherapy, surgery, and radiation, I mentally checked out. I could not think about the next steps. I was stunned, in shock, and needed a moment to digest it all. My first reaction after being diagnosed with breast cancer was not apostasy. I, however, desperately needed to talk with God, tell my mom, and research all that he had shared. What is triple-negative breast cancer? I thought breast cancer was breast cancer. How did I get this?

According to the Triple Negative Breast Cancer Foundation, "a triple-negative breast cancer diagnosis means that the offending tumor is estrogen receptor-negative, progesterone receptor-negative, and HER2-negative, thus the name 'triple-negative breast cancer.'"[1] My surgeon explained it this way, "think of a cell having three tentacles — estrogen, progesterone, and Herceptin. A triple-negative cell is minus all three of these hormones. Triple-negative breast cancer is not a hormonally based cancer, and therefore, it is not treated with hormones. It is an aggressive form of breast cancer. Thus, depending on the stage of the tumor, the treatment can be aggressive.

When the doctor shared the results, I was alone. No family member or friend had accompanied me. As I sat there, in my thoughts, I did not blame God, nor did I abandon my religious beliefs. It never crossed my mind to ask God the proverbial question, "Why me?" Thankfully, I was not afraid. I knew I had to do something. I had to decide on treatment, but not today. Philippians 4:6-7 tells us, "Be anxious for nothing, but in everything by prayer and supplication, with thanksgiving, let your requests be made known to God; and the peace of God, which surpasses all understanding, will guard your hearts and minds through Christ Jesus." God tells us to bring everything to Him, to be patient, and to wait on Him. Without realizing it, I had done this. I made no treatment decision that day. The peace of God was with me. It's amazing how much you retain when you spend time in His Word. You truly become a doer and not just a reader or hearer of the Word!

To break the silence, the doctor began talking about the next steps. I listened and tuned him out simultaneously. I had not prepared for this devastating news and really just wanted to leave the room. "I won't make any decisions today," I said. He suggested that I schedule an appointment for the following week to discuss the next steps. Trying not to wear my emotions on my face, I exited his office and the building just as I entered on autopilot. I sat in my car, and through my tears, I said a prayer. I then made three phone calls, first, to my mom. Second, to Raymond, a former boyfriend, traveling companion, and dear friend I have known since August 2000. Third, to Tommy, a childhood friend I have known since I was 13 years old.

Following those calls, I started my car and headed back to work. Now don't get me wrong, I was not stoic. I was optimistic, and I certainly had concerns. As I knew it, my world had changed in an instant, and I did not know what the future held for me. However, like it or not, I had a choice to be sad, depressed, or take God at His Word and reach for His righteous right hand. I chose to trust in my Lord and Savior, my rock and foundation, and appreciate the people He would position along the way to support and care for me throughout this mesmerizing dance.

Two years before my diagnosis, I began attending Bible study through Biblical Business Training (BBT) at Worldwide Technology on Friday mornings. The Bible study sessions, coupled with my daily study of His Word and daily meditation, prepared me for this moment. I could trust God because I spent time with Him daily. I knew no matter what I had or would experience I could stand on His promises; I would not be alone. He would comfort me. I knew God would not allow me to endure more than I could handle, and I would stand victorious.

The story of Job tells how God allowed Satan to cause the death of Job's family members and the loss of his property. My story certainly does not compare to Job's, but like Job, I, too, was resilient in the face of adversity and trials. Satan brought affliction into Job's life by attacking his character. Satan thought that by taking away all that Job loved and cherished would weaken his faith and that Job would lose trust in and denounce God. He did not. Despite it all, Job 1:20 states that after learning of his losses, "Then Job arose, tore his robe, and shaved his head, and he fell to the ground and worshipped." When Satan did not get the desired results, he attacked Job's health and "…struck him with painful boils from the sole of his feet to the crown of his head" (Job 2:7). Still, Job did not curse God. Even when his wife said, "Do you still hold fast to your integrity? Curse God and die" (v.9)! Job's response was, "…Shall we indeed accept good from God, and shall we not accept adversity? In all this, Job did not sin with his lips" (v.10). Three of Job's friends learned of his plight and believed this adversity resulted from sinful behavior, citing that God only punishes the wicked. However, this was far from the truth. Matthew 5:45 states, "He causes His sun to rise on the evil and the good and sends rain on the righteous and the unrighteous."

It is easy to follow, trust, and believe God when all is going well in life. Faith is on trial and reveals itself when adversity strikes in events such as job loss, death of a loved one, financial burdens, and an unfavorable health report. I honestly was able to see my faith in action when I received this grave diagnosis. God, however, knew the outcome. I did not. I did not know it then, but I later realized my experience was not only to glorify God but to help me grow stronger in my faith. I did not know how I would handle a life-threatening situation. I, however, had a firsthand view of what God already knew. Was I afraid? Yes, and no. I was uneasy knowing I had two cancerous tumors in my body. However, I was more concerned about the many unknowns, especially the things I could not control and questions I could not answer. Questions such as how would my body respond to chemotherapy? Will it work? Will I live? Will I die? I was dependent on God. So, I changed the focus of my spiritual attitude. I told myself I would live because God's Word said, "... By His stripes, I am healed" (Isaiah 53:5). Believing this, I was able to relax in one of my favorite scriptures, Isaiah 41:10. I was able to walk the talk of my faith!

Adversity — life's challenges — come in many forms, and the devil often is the culprit in this fallen world. However, I knew the enemy could not do anything to me without my Father's permission. On the other hand, "Satan has total access to an unbeliever, limited only by the prayers of God's faithful people."[2] When this is understood, we know God will turn Satan's evil doings around for God's purpose. We have to maintain our faith and not lose hope. God did not say His children would not experience trials and tribulations, but He does promise VICTORIES!

Moment of Clarity
Once I accepted Jesus Christ as my Lord and Savior, I became an enemy of the enemy - Satan. While Satan is roaming the earth looking to kill, steal, and destroy as he did to Job, Satan had to get permission from God to attack me. Although God allowed cancer to enter my body, there was joy in knowing 1) Jesus said, "By His stripes, I am healed...." (Isaiah 53:5). These words affirmed that I would be okay, 2) God had prepared me for this moment. I had spent time in and trusted God's Word, and 3) God did not give me breast cancer. He gave me a testimony! I knew I would be victorious whether He left me here on earth or took me home to glory!

Reflection

This is a moment for you to reflect on the "joy in your dance." Journal the experience: Where were you when you received troubling news? What were you doing? How did you respond? How did you feel when you realized it was nobody but God? Who did you tell?

_____

_____

_____

_____

_____

_____

_____

_____

_____

_____

_____

_____

_____

_____

_____

_____

_____

_____

_____

_____

_____

_____

CHAPTER 2 ~ Joy in My Dance

_____
_____
_____
_____
_____
_____
_____
_____
_____
_____
_____
_____
_____
_____
_____
_____
_____
_____
_____
_____
_____
_____
_____
_____
_____
_____
_____
_____

Reflection Questions for Discussion
1. Who is God to you? Who are you to God?
2. Do you spend time in God's Word? Do you find comfort in God's Word?
3. When you are experiencing a crisis, do you apply God's Word to the situation? Why or why not? (Reference Isaiah 43:26, Isaiah 55:11)What will you do differently?
4. What's your moment of clarity?

_____

_____

_____

_____

_____

_____

_____

_____

_____

_____

_____

_____

_____

_____

_____

_____

_____

_____

_____

_____

_____

_____

_____

_____

_____

_____

_____

_____

_____

_____

_____

_____

_____

_____

_____

_____

_____

_____

_____

_____

_____

_____

_____

_____

_____

_____

_____

_____

_____

_____

_____

_____

_____

_____

CHAPTER 3

Somebody's Gotta Have Some Sense

For all that is in the world—
the lust of the flesh, the lust of the eyes, and the pride of life
— is not of the Father but is of the world.
~ 1 John 2:16 ~

You shall not tempt the Lord your God.
~ Luke 4:12 ~

When Jesus was in the wilderness, he prayed and fasted for forty days. Knowing Jesus was hungry, Satan tried to tempt Him (Luke 4:1-13). Immediately Satan questioned Jesus' authority by trying to tempt Him to turn stone to bread (lust of the flesh). Next, he offered Jesus the kingdoms of the world if He would worship him (lust of the eyes). And lastly, he requested Jesus to jump off the pinnacle of a temple (pride of life). With each challenge, Jesus quoted scripture leading with the words, "It is written." In His final statement to the devil, Jesus said, "It has been said, 'You shall not tempt the Lord your God.'" This tells me God is to be trusted, not tested. What an example Jesus set for us to follow.

I knew I was going to be victorious over cancer from the moment I was diagnosed. I also knew I had to do my part in the process, temporarily forgoing social events and activities. When the chemotherapy sessions began, I was hesitant to be around people for several reasons, mainly because of my compromised immune system. I did not want to put myself at risk of infection.

For years, I actively participated in several professional organizations. At the time of my diagnosis, I was the immediate past president of the National Black MBA Association—St. Louis Chapter (NBMBAA-STL), and the program quality director for District 8 Toastmasters. Both organizations required a great deal of interaction with people. I needed to be careful with my health because triple-negative breast cancer is aggressive, so my oncologist treated it aggressively. Following each round of chemo, I received the Neulasta patch, which is a "man-made protein that stimulates the growth of white blood cells to decrease the incidence of infection during chemotherapy."[1] An injector would release the protein 27-hours after treatment to help rebuild my immune system. Since my immune system was compromised, I limited contact with people to avoid catching a cold or the flu. I maintained a healthy diet, managed my stress level, and did not intentionally expose myself to smokers. I listened to my body. For the most part, outside of the home, I limited my activities to two places, church, and Bible study. At church during prayer time, Bishop Jones would say, "Take your neighbor's hand" or "Turn to your neighbor." My neighbors to my left and right were always my mom and my cousin Dyane. Every Sunday, I sat between them. I knew I was covered but did not want to unnecessarily put myself at risk of infection, so I exercised caution using the wisdom and discernment God gave me.

Several weeks into my treatment, my mother had an unexpected accident. I was sitting in my office when I heard a squeal from my mom, followed by a loud and heavy bump. Rising quickly from my seat, I ran to the master bedroom and found that the door to the room was partially blocked and saw my mom lying on the floor with a 5 x 3-foot mahogany French Chester dresser over her. She said, "I cannot move." As I made my way into the room with urgency, I observed that the sweaters and shelves had slid out, and the four Chester drawers were resting on her legs. Fortunately, I could flip the Chester to one side and move the drawers enough for her to slide from underneath. Unable to stand, she was able to slide to the oversized peach loveseat by the window. I assisted her onto the seat and placed pillows under her left leg to keep it elevated. I went downstairs and returned with an icepack to minimize any swelling.

"What happened," I asked? Thinking, "we need to go to the hospital," while she spoke. "Well," she said, "I was attempting to dust the top of the Chester and did not want to disturb you, so I opened the Chester doors, stepped up on the stool, and pulled on the top to lift and balance myself." As I spoke, I could not help but notice that one leg seemed to be swelling. At that moment, the telephone rang. I stood up and walked to the right along the foot of the bed, avoiding the chaos on the floor, to answer the phone. It was Raymond.

Just arriving in town from Columbus, OH, Raymond said, "Hey, I'm about 10 minutes away. Do you want me to stop to pick up anything?" "No," I replied. "What's going on?" he asked with a concerned tone in his voice. I guess he sensed something was wrong. I began to tell him what happened when he interrupted me and asked, "Can she walk at all?" "Not really," I said. "I'm almost there. If you can, help her down the steps. We'll get her to the hospital," he continued. Putting pressure on her right leg, we made it down the steps. My mother was able to sit and slide into the back seat of the vehicle. Once at the hospital, using a wheelchair, we ushered her into the emergency room waiting area, checked her in, and waited. Finally, after some time, her vital signs were taken by a nurse. Shortly thereafter, she was taken to a room where the attending nurse prepped her for an x-ray. The results, a fractured knee that required a temporary stabilizing brace with the use of crutches. My asset was now a liability.

While at the hospital, the attending nurse learned of my cancer diagnosis and immediately had me put on a face mask. Because of my pending surgery, she felt the hospital was the last place I should be and urged me to go home. The nurse cautioned me about exposing myself unnecessarily to germs. I did not want to leave my mother, but Raymond and I left the hospital at my mom's urging with great hesitation. Before leaving, however, I made a quick call. I was assured of two things. First, my mom was not alone, and second, my cousin Dyane had arrived.

My mother's accident rendered her semi-immobile. While at home, she was confined to the first floor as she could not put weight on her left leg. Moreover, it would have been quite challenging and dangerous for her to navigate the 14 steps leading upstairs. Now, the family room temporarily became a makeshift bedroom, and the half bath on the main level became a shared space. The accident happened over the Fourth of July weekend, just four days before having a double mastectomy on July 6. Interestingly, everyone focused on my positive attitude and the strength I displayed from the start of my dance. I, however, also witnessed the strength and determination of my mom during her dance. She did not complain. Determined to heal and regain the strength in her leg to walk, she was self-sufficient downstairs, and she only needed assistance when requesting upstairs items.

Moment of Clarity

Jesus' confrontation with Satan gave me a sense of assurance. My mom and I could have seen her fall as a major setback, but we did not. We stayed focused on God, stayed in His Word, and made the necessary adjustments. Knowing that with God's help, we would come through this. What the enemy meant for evil, God worked it out for good. God had us covered, and we both had to be careful and avoid placing ourselves in harm's way by using good judgment. In the infamous words of my cousin Mattie, "Somebody's gotta have some sense."

Reflection

This is a time for you to reflect on your "gotta have some sense" moment(s). Journal the experience: What was the situation? How did you respond? What adjustments did you make in order to keep things moving?

_____

_____

_____

_____

_____

CHAPTER 3 ~ Somebody's Gotta Have Some Sense

_____

_____

_____

_____

_____

_____

_____

_____

_____

_____

_____

_____

_____

_____

_____

_____

_____

_____

_____

_____

_____

_____

_____

_____

_____

_____

_____

_____

_____

_____
_____
_____
_____
_____
_____

Reflection Questions for Discussion

1. Your plan was in place, then something happened. What happened? Did you feel paralyzed? How quickly did you adjust?
2. When things don't go as planned, are you flexible? Do you turn to God's Word? Do you find comfort in God's promises?
3. When you feel overwhelmed or anxious what do you do? (Reference Isaiah 26:3)
4. What's your moment of clarity?

_____
_____
_____
_____
_____
_____
_____
_____
_____
_____
_____
_____

CHAPTER 3 ~ Somebody's Gotta Have Some Sense

_____

_____

_____

_____

_____

_____

_____

_____

_____

_____

_____

_____

_____

_____

_____

_____

_____

_____

_____

_____

_____

_____

_____

_____

_____

_____

_____

_____

_____

_____

Section Two

Stretching My Hands to God (*Praising*)

Yet in all these things we are more than conquerors through Him who loved us. For I am persuaded that neither death nor life, nor angels nor principalities nor powers, nor things present nor things to come, nor height nor depth, nor any other created thing, shall be able to separate us from the love of God which is in Christ Jesus our Lord.
~ Romans 8:37-39 ~

Chapter 4

Model for Jesus

Abide in Me, and I in you.
As the branch cannot bear fruit of itself, unless it abides in the
vine, neither can you, unless you abide in Me.
I am the vine; you are the branches.
He who abides in Me, and I in him, bears much fruit;
for without Me you can do nothing.
~ John 15:4-5 ~

Let your light so shine before men,
that they may see your good works and glorify your Father in
Heaven.
~ Matthew 5:16 ~

During a drought, God instructed the Prophet Elijah to travel to Zarephath, where He says, "I have commanded a widow there to provide for you" (1 King 17:9). The widow, whose name is unknown, is unaware of this command. Nonetheless, she honored Elijah's request for water and a "morsel of bread" even though it was the last of what she had (vv. 10-12). Through her obedience, the God of Israel blessed her abundantly. While Elijah was not an angel, he was a prophet, and he walked with God. Hebrews 13:1-2 says, "Let brotherly love continue. Do not forget to entertain strangers, for by so doing, some have unwittingly entertained angels."

During February, so many things occurred before the start of my first round of chemo. I had changed my breast surgeon and found a new one at Barnes Jewish Hospital. While my chart followed me, the process of answering questions and the examination of my left breast and left underarm started, yet again. Additionally, I had to take another series of tests: Mammogram/Ultrasound, Magnetic Resonance Imaging (MRI), Computed Tomography

(CT), and a bone scan. Leading up to the start of chemo, nearly every hour of the day, I felt like I was either at a doctor's office or the hospital.

Nonetheless, I stayed abreast of every stage of the process. From day one, I never went to an appointment without questions for my doctors. Further, I did not leave without a clear understanding of why this, as opposed to that. I was vigilant about my treatment options and knowing what it meant for my healing and recovery. More importantly, I maintained a positive, friendly, and victorious attitude. As an ambassador for Christ, you never know who's watching you. I had to represent!

There are four identified stages in cancer — stage 0 to stage 4. Wait. I know what you're thinking. There are five stages. True. Stages 2 and 3, however, are grouped. This is known as "regional spread" cancer. According to an article by Ty Bollinger, "Understanding the 4 Stages of Cancer," he states, "Stages 2 and 3 indicate a serious cause for concern, but the cancer has not spread to other organs in the body."[1] Based on the size and location of my two masses, doctors initially diagnosed me with stage 3 breast cancer. They were concerned that cancer in my lymph nodes had metastasized — traveled — to other parts of my body through the bloodstream. Using a "contrast agent" or dye injected into my body, the MRI would provide a 3-D image of my body's non-bony and soft tissues. This would allow the doctor to see if cancer appeared elsewhere. I had to lie on my stomach and be perfectly still for about 45 minutes in this noisy tubular structure. Of course, I could breathe, but I could not move to ensure a clear image. It was difficult not to move, so I quietly sang songs of praise in my head to help pass the time and stay connected to God. I focused on Him and not on my situation or the repetitive tapping and thumping noise coming from the machine.

By now, I had met the medical oncologist — a doctor who specializes in treating cancer with chemotherapy, hormone therapy, targeted therapy, or immunotherapy — who ordered another set of tests for me to take. Two days before the start of chemotherapy, my schedule called for a bone scan and a CT scan. Two hours before the bone scan, the nurse injected radioactive material into my vein that traveled through the bloodstream. This test is designed to detect cancerous cells that had metastasized to the bone from the breast. I had to wait two hours before I took the actual test, so I left the Nuclear Medicine area and headed to Radiology for the CT scan. This scan would show cross-sectional images of my bones, organs, and tissues. After the CT scan, I returned to Nuclear Medicine for the bone scan. Truthfully, it was a bit nerve-racking waiting for the test results. I tried to wait calmly, but my nerves took over, and diarrhea reared its head. I could not stop thinking about this unknown. I tried to be strong. Plus, I knew my mom was feeding off of my energy and mood. I repeatedly said to myself, "Jacquie, you are not in control. God is. You turned it over to Him. Leave it with Him." The test results showed no cancer in other parts of my body. Whew. Praise God!

As you can imagine, during my appointments, I encountered all levels of people who worked in the hospital, including patients and their guests. There was a pleasant exchange in each encounter. I was always full of energy and smiles, emitting the strength and favor of God. On the evening of my MRI, I sat in a dimly lit waiting area with two other women. One lady wore an examination gown just as I did. Besides exchanging a pleasant greeting, she was quiet and focused on the magazine positioned on her lap. I did learn, however, that she, too, had been diagnosed with breast cancer and was waiting for an MRI. The other young lady was waiting for her son, who had been diagnosed with a form of brain cancer. I don't recall his whole story, but one thing was clear she was his cheerleader and stood with the angels to comfort him. We talked about God and our faith as we waited.

One day, as I sat in the hospital's waiting area across from the Siteman Cancer Center for treatment, I looked around and noticed there were many people also waiting. Along with my entourage, I sat away from the check-in window, waiting for my electronic device to vibrate, signaling it was time for my blood draw. While waiting, I noticed a gentleman looking for the restroom. He asked me where the restrooms were located. I told him he was in the right section. When he returned to the waiting area, we started talking. He said he had been diagnosed with throat cancer and was at the hospital alternating between chemotherapy and radiation five days a week. He went home on weekends, which was about three hours away. In sharing his story, he told me his wife had also been recently diagnosed with cancer. I do not know if he was a believer, but he was optimistic about their treatment and recovery. Sadly, I later realized I may have missed the opportunity to minister to a non-believer. I should have asked. Nonetheless, I could go on and on with similar stories as believers love to talk and share God's goodness. To me, this is "faith in action," where believers don't focus on the situation but God's faithfulness and goodness.

Speaking of "faith in action," you never know who's watching you. After checking in for my first round of chemo, I passed a nurse I had met during an earlier visit with the breast surgeon. I was sure she did not remember my name, nor I hers. I later learned; however, she remembered my positive attitude. After we exchanged pleasantries and briefly talked about the procedure I was having done, she escorted me into a room where I would meet the surgeon and the team performing the needle biopsy on the right breast. The first words the doctor said were, "We've heard a lot of good things about you." Everyone agreed with her. I imagined the doctor was referring to my bubbly personality and friendly, positive attitude. I chose to believe I had exuded "faith in action," salt of the earth. I imagined Jesus smiling and His light shining brightly in and through me.

Moment of Clarity
Dr. Charles Stanley says, "The only way we can play a significant role in the kingdom of God is to allow Jesus to live His life in and through us."[2] We may be the only Jesus some people see. Represent Him well. Model for Jesus!

This is a time for you to reflect on your "faith in action" moment(s). Journal the experience: Where were you? What were you doing? Describe the situation and your response. How did you feel? Who did you tell?

_____

_____

_____

_____

_____

_____

_____

_____

_____

_____

_____

_____

_____

_____

_____

_____

_____

_____

_____

_____

_____

_____

_____

_____

_____

_____

_____

_____

_____

_____

Reflection Questions for Discussion
1. Do others see you as a person of faith?
2. Do you believe you are "the salt of the earth?" (Reference Matthew 5:13, Colossians 4:6) What does this statement mean to you?
3. Give an example of your "faith in action."
4. What's your moment of clarity?

_____

_____

_____

_____

_____

_____

_____

_____

_____

_____

_____

_____\

_____

_____

_____

Chapter 5

Dog is God Spelled Backwards

For as the sash clings to the waist of a man, so I have caused the
whole household of Israel and the whole household of Judah to
cling to Me, says the LORD, that they may become My people,
for renown, for praise, and for glory...
~ Jeremiah 13:11 ~

Jonathan, son of King Saul of Israel, loved David, whom Samuel had anointed as the future king. Although King Saul resented David, scripture states that "...Jonathan and David made a covenant, because he loved him as his own soul" (1 Samuel 18:3). Risking his life, Jonathan did all he could to protect David from death at the hands of his father, King Saul. This "bromance" reminds me of two characteristics found in dogs. First, dogs are loyal companions. Much like Jonathan with David, dogs are protective and compassionate, especially toward their owner. Second, no matter how you treat a dog, they remain loving, forgiving, and continue to show unconditional love toward you. Although King Saul's jealousy of David led him on an unyielding path to kill him, David remained respectful to the king out of his obedience to God.

In March 2014, a new male figure joined my household. He is smart, funny, and was never going to be a financial contributor to my household, but I've learned an invaluable lesson from him. I acquired this six-month-old white with blond patches Poodle, Shih-Tzu, and Jack-Russell mixed companion from a coworker. My coworker already had six dogs that did not include the new litter of three. She definitely did not want any more dogs, so she let people know they were – Free! This appealed to me. I wanted a dog but could not bring myself to buy a dog. I'm old school. Growing up in New Jersey, I was accustomed to people giving dogs away. It was not uncommon for someone to say, "Hey, my dog had a litter of pups, want one?" My colleague sent me pictures of three adorable pups. We arranged for a visit so I could meet the little ones, one male and two females.

The day arrived for me to meet the pups. With all of the characteristics of a Jack-Russell, the male entered first and immediately started exploring the environment. His sisters followed him, one with white curly hair like a Poodle and the other with hair like a Shih-Tzu. Their blond patches were not very prominent. Both were curious but hesitant. I interacted with and watched the three of them and quickly noticed that the male appeared to be on a mission. It was as if he knew he was moving and decided that my home would be his new home. He chose me and started to block or limit my interaction with the girls. And while I chose him, I immediately reached out to a cousin in New Jersey to see if she wanted a puppy, and my mom spoke with a friend in St. Louis about them. It was settled. Bunny, who has characteristics of Shih-Tzu, resides in St. Louis. Daisy lives in Union, New Jersey.

The male, whom I named Barkley, lived with me. He was full of energy and a ball of fun! Little did I know, he would live up to the first four letters of his name. He was indeed a barker. He barked at everyone and everything, and Barkley followed me everywhere — to the point of driving me bananas. There was no longer any privacy in the house; every room belonged to him. I initially thought he was getting accustomed to a new environment, but as time passed, I realized this was one of his many traits. If I sat down, it was Barkley's opportunity to jump into my lap and sit too. Never could I sit at my office desk alone. He would position himself behind me, in my seat, preventing me from being able to comfortably sit back. Barkley was also extraordinarily protective and comforting. This behavior was evident when I began chemotherapy. He never wanted to leave my side. I would have to force him to go downstairs to eat or go for a walk with my mother. I don't know at what point Barkley became excessively clingy. When I awoke from a nap, I would often find him curled up next to me and staring. He acted as if we were one. I wish I had paid closer attention to his behaviors.

I was still working when I began my treatments on Friday, March 4, 2016. Every three weeks, I would take a Friday off for treatment. This routine would continue until June 17. Following each round of chemo, the nurse attached the Neulasta patch below and to the right of my belly button. Twenty-seven hours after chemo on a Saturday evening, the patch would release its contents. Nothing prepared me for the effects of the shot. I recall waking up on Sunday morning, moving around, and feeling a little light-headed as I tried to dress for church. By Sunday evening, all I wanted to do and could do was snuggle up next to my mom on the sofa with Barkley by my side.

By the time Monday morning rolled around for work, I felt like every bone and joint in my body was being attacked. I called on Jesus for His Strength and kept it moving. These particular Mondays were extremely challenging because my equilibrium was off, causing instability. I can remember slowly climbing the steps from the lower level parking garage and holding the rails tightly to prevent falling. When I returned home from work, all I could do was go to bed and sleep to avoid the immense discomfort. Everything seemed to be in slow motion, except Barkley, who never left my side.

The Neulasta shot was a necessary evil designed to rebuild my weakened immune system. This, coupled with chemo, left me with no appetite for about four to five days. During that time, my tongue would turn white, and nothing tasted good. Eating was like trying to push hay down a parched throat, so I drank lots of water and could only stomach an Ensure or Boost. At about day four or five, my appetite returned, and my taste buds came alive. I could eat like usual. From that point, I knew I had a solid two weeks of feeling pretty good. However, I noticed I became a little more fatigued with every round of chemo, even though I felt pretty good.

Every three weeks, I had chemotherapy treatments. On the morning of my first round of chemo, guess who came uninvited into the bathroom following my shower? Barkley! I could barely apply lotion to my body because he felt he needed to be next to me to make me aware of his presence. A part of Barkley's body had to touch mine. A paw resting on my foot. His back against my leg. Or, he would lightly brush his nose against my leg. Anything to let me know he was there. He was truly a huge comfort throughout my cancer treatment, and it saddens me to write that he is no longer with me.

To make a long story short, I made two mistakes on October 10, 2017. I failed to lock my front door after a friend entered the house, and upon exiting the house through the kitchen, I put the house alarm on "away" as opposed to "stay." I can only imagine Barkley staring at the door, finding it hard to believe I would leave him to go to a meeting. Once he moved, the alarm sounded. After several attempts to reach me, the alarm company contacted the police. Upon checking the perimeter, the police were able to enter the home through the front door. It was unlocked. With the door wide open, Barkley ran out. To this day, despite him having an implanted chip and a visible name tag with my contact information — and a reward for his return – he has not been returned. I pray that someone has him and is taking great care of him…. So much personality!

Moment of Clarity
If we paid attention to God's creation, we would see that He lets us know He is ever-present: the morning dew, sunshine, a light breeze against our skin, flowers, birds, etc. With that thought, the message was simple and clear. Barkley was clinging to me the way God wants us to cling to Him!

November 14, 2020, I acquired a three-plus-year-old Poodle, Shih-Tzu mix from a family looking to rehome him. I renamed him, Hudson. His features and character are similar to Barkley's. He loves to snuggle, touch, follow me around the house, and he never meets strangers. In his mind, he knows everyone in and out of the neighborhood. Like most dogs, he loves to play in the leaves and the snow. What he does not like is the rain. He associates rain with thunder and lightning, and there is nowhere to hide. With every storm, he starts to pant and tremble and knows the safest place for him to be is with me. With every storm, he's learned to come to me first. Here is yet another lesson, when the storms of life come, God wants us to turn to Him first. Our shoulders are not broad enough to carry the weight of fear, anxiety, confusion, disappointment, etc. He invites us to turn to Him first, the author and finisher of our faith. He says, "cast all your care upon Him, for He cares for you" 1 Peter 5:7.

Reflection

This is a moment for you to reflect on "what gives you comfort." Journal the experience: Describe the situation. Where were you? What were you doing? How did you respond?

_____

_____

_____

_____

_____

_____

_____

_____

_____

_____

_____

_____

_____

_____

_____

_____

_____

_____

_____

_____

_____

_____

Reflection Questions for Discussion
1. When you are in your valley moment, where do you find comfort?
2. As you reflect on question one, are there lessons learned that reflect God's desired relationship with you?
3. In your valley, how do you apply God's Word to the situation?
4. What's your moment of clarity?

_____

_____

_____

_____

_____

_____

_____

_____

_____

_____

_____

_____

_____

_____

_____

Chapter 6

With Me Always

Have I not commanded you?
Be strong and of good courage; do not be afraid,
nor be dismayed, for the Lord your God is
with you wherever you go.
~ Joshua 1:9 ~

Shortly after Sarah gave birth to Isaac, Hagar, Abraham's concubine, and their son Ishmael was exiled to the desert. Although her situation looked bleak and her future uncertain, an Angel of the LORD said to her, "I will multiply your descendants exceedingly, so that they shall not be counted for multitude" (Genesis 16:10). God promised her that Ishmael would raise up a great nation of his own. Hagar's story is a great reminder that God knows us, sees us, and cares about His children. No matter what we go through or experience, "The angel of the LORD encamps all around those who [reverence] Him, And delivers them" (Psalms 34:7).

The day my breast surgeon and I discussed the next steps in my treatment, I realized I would go through several surgeries, namely, an implantable port, double mastectomy, and if I elected to do so, reconstructive surgery. The breast reconstruction surgery would not begin until many months after the completion of the radiation treatments. Okay, one surgery at a time.

Approximately two weeks before my first round of chemo, a device about the size of a quarter called a port-a-cath was to be surgically placed just under my skin, below my right shoulder blade. This temporary port was to administer chemotherapy medicines intravenously through a special needle. A soft, thin tube called a catheter connected the port to a large vein in my chest. Now that you know what the port is and its purpose, let me tell you what was most interesting about the day of this outpatient procedure that let me know God was present.

My mom, Aunt Catherine, and I arrived at the hospital at approximately 6:15 a.m. for a 7:30 a.m. outpatient procedure. As I checked in at the registration desk, the administrator asked a few questions, verified my insurance information, had me sign a couple of electronic documents, and instructed me to have a seat in the waiting area. Ten minutes later, I was ushered into the OR prep area and advised that my guests would be able to join me after I was prepped for surgery. Walking down the corridor, I was surprised to see so many people prepped or being prepped for surgery as the main waiting area gave no indication.

As I laid in the hospital bed dressed in a stylish light blue floral hospital gown, donning a blue paperweight hospital cap, my mom and aunt were escorted to my now crowded space. Shortly afterward, the anesthesiologist entered and introduced himself and asked me a series of questions. The two questions that stood out were, "Ms. Vick, when was your last cycle?" To which I responded, "It's been more than ten years. If it came back now, I would be pissed." We chuckled, and he continued. "Any chance you could be pregnant?" An emphatic "No. Not unless God is being funny." Then he said, "Well, you know Sarah had a baby in her 90's."

As soon as the anesthesiologist referenced that biblical story, God's Spirit, which dwells within me, put me at peace. I knew God was with me. He said in His Word, "I will not leave you nor forsake you" (Joshua 1:5 and Hebrews 13:5). Just as He assured Joshua and Hagar, He assured me, and I knew I would come through the procedure with no problems. My thoughts were interrupted as the nurse began to administer pre-anesthesia medication. I heard the nurse say, "We'll see you shortly," as I was wheeled out of the room for a 45 to 60-minute procedure. Everything was seamless. Praise God!

Moment of Clarity

My heavenly Father used the anesthesiologist to let me know He was with me through the procedure. In my moment of clarity, I recalled a sermon delivered by Bishop Jones where he focused on Jesus being a friend. He said, "This relationship is personal. God's love for me is unconditional and everlasting. Jesus is my partner; He calls me 'friend' (John 15:15). I got it like that!" What a friend we have in Jesus! And like a true and faithful friend, He is with us always!

Reflection

This is a moment for you to reflect on "the time(s) you knew God was with you." Journal the experience: Where were you? What were you doing? How did you respond? How did you feel when you realized it was nobody but God? Who did you tell?

_____

_____

_____

_____

_____

_____

_____

_____

_____

_____

_____

_____

_____

_____

_____

_____

Reflection Questions for Discussion
1. Where are you in your faith walk? Can you confidently stand on God's promise that he will be with you always?
2. Has there ever been a time where you wondered if God had forsaken you?
3. When you are experiencing a crisis, do you apply God's Word to the situation? Why or why not? (Reference Isaiah 43:26)
4. What's your moment of clarity?

_____

_____

_____

_____

_____

_____

_____

_____

_____

_____

_____

_____

_____

_____

_____

_____

_____

_____

_____

_____

Section Three

Turning My Mourning into Dancing (Worshiping)

Many, O LORD my God, are Your wonderful works
Which You have done; *And Your thoughts toward us
Cannot be recounted to You in order; If* I would declare and
speak *of them, They are more than can be numbered.*
~ Psalm 40:5 ~

Chapter 7

Count It All Joy

My brethren, count it all joy when you fall into various trials,
knowing that the testing of your faith produces patience.
But let patience have its perfect work,
that you may be perfect and complete, lacking nothing.
~ James 1:2-4 ~

The Bible tells us that we will experience trials and tribulations on earth and provides several accounts of believers who endured them. One story that stands out for me is the story of Joseph. God gave Joseph a vision. He shared it with his father and brothers. It, however, was troubling to his brothers. As a result, when the opportunity presented itself, the brothers plotted against Joseph and ultimately sold him into slavery. After earning favor with Potiphar, Potiphar's wife made advances towards Joseph, but he rebuffed her. Because of this, she lied about Joseph, and he was imprisoned for two years. Joseph could have lost faith because the manifestation of God's promise had not come into fruition, but he did not. Instead, he held on to the vision that God had given him. What Joseph's brothers meant for evil, God meant for good. After interpreting the king's dream, Joseph was released from prison. The king appointed him second in command over the kingdom, where he would now plan to save his people from a drought. Like Joseph, we have to hold on to God's promises. "There is nothing joyful about trials, in and of themselves. There is no value in suffering for its own sake. God uses both trials and suffering [so that we can see our level of faith and] so that we may learn to patiently endure."[1]

I am a very strategic person, in big and small things. For example, if I have errands to run, I precisely map out my directions before leaving home. It has to make sense. No zigzagging for me. I hit all stops in one direction before heading in another direction. I share this with you to preface what I will tell you about an appointment

I scheduled on my first day of chemotherapy. I intended to plan, minimize, and maximize my time at the hospital. Let me back up and tell the story. A few days following my MRI, my breast surgeon called me to share the test results. She said the test revealed a dark spot in my right breast, and she wanted to order a needle biopsy. My strategic mental wheels immediately began to turn. I stated I wanted to schedule the procedure on the same day as my first round of chemo to avoid making an extra trip to the hospital. I subsequently received a call from an appointment scheduler. We added the needle biopsy to my schedule: 7:30 a.m.- lab, 8 a.m. - right breast biopsy, 9:30 a.m. - an office visit with the oncologist, and 10 a.m. - chemotherapy.

Before starting each round of chemo, I had to check in for a complete blood count (CBC). The CBC allowed the doctor to monitor my blood counts because "chemotherapy drugs can damage bone marrow and stop it from producing enough red blood cells, white blood cells, and platelets. Low blood cell counts [can] put you at risk of serious complications."[2]

According to the Mayo Clinic, white blood cells help your body fight infection. A low white blood cell count (leukopenia) leaves your body more open to infection. If an infection develops, your body may be unable to fight it off. Red blood cells carry oxygen throughout your body. Your red blood cells' ability to carry oxygen is measured by the amount of hemoglobin in your blood. If your hemoglobin level is low, you are anemic, and it is much more challenging for your body to supply oxygen to your tissues. This can make you feel tired and short of breath. Platelets help your blood to clot. A low platelet count (thrombocytopenia) means your body can't stop itself from bleeding."[3]

After completing the lab work, my next stop was to meet with the surgeon who would perform the needle biopsy. As I stepped in the elevator on the 12th floor, I quickly pressed the button for the fifth floor. Once I arrived on the fifth floor and checked-in at the front desk, I was escorted to a changing room and then a small dimly lit room where I was asked to lie on a bed next to a monitor. The monitor provided a visual for the doctor to identify the exact location of the dark spot. I could also see the spot and heard the click when she clamped down to remove a tissue sample. The procedure was quick. Once done, I dressed, and off I went to meet with my oncologist and his team. Here, the nurse captured my blood pressure, height, and weight. The doctor reviewed the CBC results, checked my weight, inputted information in the computer, and sent me across the hall to the Siteman Cancer Center for chemotherapy.

This process was interesting, and I must admit, I was somewhat uneasy. All of the "unknowns" I had grappled with led up to this day, and this surreal experience was now real. To prepare for the procedure, a nurse ushered me to an area with approximately eight to ten stations, of which two had beds. I had the option of sitting up or lying down to receive my chemo. I say "my" chemo because each treatment is designed specifically to address the patient's needs. There are different chemotherapy treatments, and the hours it takes to receive chemotherapy vary.

Two consecutive days before the first day of treatment, I took two rounds of steroid tablets. I was required to take these tablets before each treatment. At the start of each treatment round, I received a liquid steroid and anti-nausea drugs to prevent an allergic reaction to the chemotherapy medicines. The treatments were administered in intervals of thirty minutes. For the next hour, I received docetaxel, which can cause total body hair loss (head, eyelashes, eyebrows, underarm, legs, and sometimes public hair). The drug can also cause darkening and possible loss of toenails and fingernails. To minimize nail loss, for an hour, I received a cold therapy. This involved placing my hands and feet in a two-sided bag – an area for my extremities and another area filled with ice. After about two minutes, my fingers and toes were freezing. The thin hospital socks I was given to wear did not help keep my feet warm. "That's okay," I thought. "I was not prepared the first time, but trust me, I will be for the second through sixth rounds." At my following treatments, I came armed with thick socks and gloves. For an hour following the cold therapy, the drug carboplatin was administered. With this drug, I experienced a loss of appetite and a change in taste. Additionally, my tongue would turn white and remain so for approximately five days. To help prevent this, I was told to drink plenty of water. No matter how much water I drank or how much I brushed and scraped my tongue, it still turned white.

The following Monday or Tuesday evening, after my first round of chemo, I received a call from my breast surgeon with the needle biopsy results. Pre-cancer was detected in my right breast, so she said, "When we perform the mastectomy on the left breast, we will do a lumpectomy on the right." I said, "No, let's just take them both. I'm not married to either one of them." After ending the conversation, I thanked God for revealing the pre-cancer in the right breast. Had He not, down the road, I possibly would have had to repeat the entire process — and I did not ever want to relive this experience. I was at peace with my decision because I wanted to reduce the risk of a recurrence. I had met too many women who had a reoccurrence of breast cancer after 15, 20, and even 30 plus years.

I realize a decision like this would be difficult for many women — even receiving news that both breasts are cancerous can be devastating. I thank God that it wasn't difficult for me, and I was grateful that it was detected. Anything we face in life, we can "count it all joy" (James 1:2), knowing we are not alone, and that God will work things out for our good.

Moment of Clarity
I was amazed at how well I handled everything, but I knew it was God's strength, grace, and mercy that enabled me to strategically plan the events of the day and victoriously go through this process. Praise God!

Reflection

This is a time for you to reflect on your "count it all joy" moment(s). Journal the experience: Where were you? What were you doing? How did you respond? How did you feel when you realized it was nobody but God? Who did you tell?

_____

_____

_____

_____

_____

_____

_____

_____

_____

_____

_____

_____

_____

_____

_____

_____

_____

_____

_____

_____

_____

_____

Reflection Questions for Discussion
1. Talk about a time when the news received was not what you expected. Did you find joy in the situation, in spite of the circumstance?
2. Has there ever been a time that you wondered if God had forsaken you?
3. When you are experiencing a crisis, do you apply God's Word to the situation? Why or why not? (Reference Isaiah 55:11)
4. What's your moment of clarity?

_____

_____

_____

_____

_____

_____

_____

_____

_____

_____

_____

_____

_____

_____

_____

_____

_____

_____

_____

_____

Chapter 8

Inner Voice

Therefore, as the Holy Spirit says: "Today, if you hear His voice,
do not harden your hearts, as you did in the rebellion,
in the day of testing in the wilderness, where your fathers tested
and tried Me, and for forty years saw My works.
~ Hebrews 3:7-9 ~

If you love me, you will obey my commands.
~ John 14:15 ~

Throughout the Bible, we see examples of God communicating with humankind; and throughout the Bible, we see the results of obedience. God walked and talked with Adam in the Garden of Eden. God told Noah that He would send a great flood and instructed him to build an Ark. This act of obedience saved the lives of his family and two of every living creature. After fulfilling His promise of a son to Abraham and Sarah, God directed Abraham to slay His son Isaac. Moments before the slaying, an angel appeared and pointed to a ram in the bush. On a mission to persecute Christians, Saul encountered Jesus on the road to Damascus. This encounter foiled Saul's mission and changed his life forever as he became Paul and proclaimed the Gospel. Jonah traveled to Jaffa rather than to the city of Nineveh as God had instructed. Jonah did not want to prophesy in Nineveh because of "their great wickedness." When thrown overboard, Jonah was swallowed by a large fish. After three days, he was on his way to Nineveh. The point, just as God communicated with humankind then, He still does so today. We never know when or where we will hear the small still voice of God's Spirit. One thing is sure, God communicates with believers through the Holy Spirit. As we grow in God's Word and develop an intimate relationship with Him, we will become spiritually alert. Knowing this, why was I surprised when I heard His voice during round three of my chemotherapy?

Very unassumingly, about halfway through my treatment, I needed to use the restroom. Focused on the reading material I had spread over a small table in the station, I tried to maneuver getting out of my seat to go to the restroom. Not only did I have to maneuver around my materials, I had to disconnect from the station and wheel the medical equipment dispensing the medicine into the restroom. As I fiddled around with everything, I noticed a lady walking a few steps behind a nurse's assistant into the treatment area. The woman had a very vivid emotional expression on her face. It was the look of fear, distress, confusion, sadness, and loneliness. You name it. I watched the assistant usher the woman into a chair and pull the curtain around them for privacy. I could not hear what was said — nor was I trying too — but I saw the assistant leave the station and heard the lady's moans. I became sad for her, especially since no one was with her. I resumed my efforts to unhook the tubes so I could go to the restroom. Then I heard the Holy Spirit's voice say, "You need to pray with her." I sat still, stunned, and thought of my need to go to the restroom. Yet, I answered, "Who me?" I could not deny what I heard, so I panicked. I thought with all of the fluid pumping into me, I had better get to the restroom. While in the restroom, I said, "Lord, if you want me to pray with this lady, you'll have to give me the words to speak over her."

As I stepped beyond the restroom door, I looked around for the nurse's assistant who had helped the lady. I saw her, and when our eyes locked, I motioned for her to come closer. Pointing I said, "Please ask the lady you seated in that cubicle if I can pray with her." She did, and the woman's response was, "Yes." I thought I was going to faint. The assistant asked if she could be a part of the prayer. I panicked, but I knew I had to follow through with God's command. As I began to walk toward the cubicle, the grandson of another patient handed me an illustrated biblical booklet he had created. He asked me to give it to the lady. I stepped into the cubicle where the woman was located and introduced myself. I said, "The Holy Spirit told me to pray with you." I asked for her name and if she was a believer. She shared her name and simultaneously nodded her head and said, "Yes." I took a deep breath and began to pray. I don't remember what I said, but my prayers always start with acknowledging who God is, giving thanks, and asking for forgiveness before petitioning our Father for a prayer request. God did not give believers the spirit of sadness, loneliness, and all the other demonic characteristics this woman showed. Those spirits are of the enemy — Satan. When we trust and believe, we can be like Paul and know that "The Lord will rescue [us] from every evil attack..."[1]

Moment of Clarity

Openly praying for a stranger was a first for me. I believe two things happened in this encounter. First, God was testing me. Second, God knew I was spiritually alert and would be obedient to the prompting of His Spirit. I did not know if I would be obedient, but God made me aware He knew my faithfulness through this act. God gave me the strength and equipped me for His purpose!

Reflection

This is a moment for you to reflect on your "inner voice" encounter. Journal the experience: Where were you? What were you doing? How did you respond? How did you feel when you realized it was nobody but God? Who did you tell?

_____

_____

_____

_____

_____

_____

_____

_____

Reflection Questions for Discussion
1. Can you discern the voice of God? Do you seek clarity?
2. How do you know if the "inner voice" is Spirit and not flesh (a gut feeling)?
3. Has there been a time that you were instructed to do something, and you chose to ignore the prompting or did the complete opposite? What were the consequences?
4. What's your moment of clarity?

_____

_____

_____

_____

_____

_____

_____

_____

_____

_____

_____

_____

_____

_____

_____

_____

_____

_____

_____

_____

_____

Chapter 9

Battle Beautifully

The Belt of Truth
The Breastplate of Righteousness
The Shoes of Peace
The Shield of Faith
The Helmet of Salvation
The Sword of the Spirit
Through Prayer and Supplication
~ Ephesians 6:13-18 ~

There are stories in the Old and New Testament illustrating the strength of women who were victorious through the power of our Heavenly Father. These women recognized they could accomplish nothing eternal without God but could accomplish everything through God (John 15:5). The Book of Esther shows the faithfulness of Queen Esther. Haman's plot to kill all Jews in Shushan is foiled when Queen Esther prayed and devised a battle plan at the risk of her demise. Queen Esther's Uncle Mordecai reminded her that she may have been positioned in the Persian King's Palace for "such a time as this." She battled beautifully by asking the Jewish people to join her in a three-day fast. For three days and nights, the people were to neither eat nor drink. After which, she risked going before the King so that her people would not perish. God equips us for our faith walk and instructs us to put on His whole armor to be victorious against the enemy's attacks. Therefore, like Queen Esther, I had to suit up for my dance.

A woman possesses two external features that can affect her psyche if lost: hair and breasts. I was in the process of losing both. With hair loss, women can sometimes feel embarrassed, ashamed, stressed out, and even depressed. Based on a few discussions I had, some women equated the absence of breasts to having a hysterectomy. A woman's breasts are the physical parts that "makes her a woman," and her hair is her "crown." While I refused to let my hair and breasts define me, I realized that being diagnosed with cancer made me vulnerable to the enemy. What better time for the enemy to attack me, play with my emotions, and cause me to question my faith and trust in God? These thoughts emerged after I read and discussed, *Fervent*, a book by Priscilla Shirer, with my Friendly Temple Book Club. And again, following a discussion on spiritual warfare with my BBT Bible study group. I was not intentionally going to be a target for the enemy. So, how did I guard myself against the tactics of the enemy? Every morning, I proclaimed my Confession of Faith, and I would specifically restate, "*Greater is He that is in me than he that is in the world. I cancel every demonic assignment and bind every demon that comes against me. I loose the anointing of God to remove every burden and destroy every yoke in my life.*" Additionally, I stayed in God's Word and wore His armor for His protection and to strengthen my relationship with Him.

Every Sunday, I attended church, and every Friday, I attended Bible study. I welcomed being in fellowship with my brothers and sisters in Christ; scripture instructs us to "not forsake the assembling of ourselves together" (Hebrews 10:25). Scripture also reminds us that, "As iron sharpens iron, so a man sharpens the countenance of his friend" (Proverbs 27:17). While I continued to dress, put on makeup, wear a wig, and, occasionally, a scarf, I was mindful of who and whose I was. I was not trying to cover up my dance. I was a walking testimony, and I knew that "[my] beauty should not come from outward adornments, such as wearing elaborate hairstyles, gold jewelry, or fine clothes. Rather, it should come from within — [my] inner self, the unfading beauty of a gentle and quiet spirit, which is of great worth in God's sight" (1Peter 3:3-4). Additionally, I was careful about the company I kept. My inner circle of family and friends were those who stood in agreement with me. Unlike those who thought I was sick and dying, they believed I was "healed and whole" because of their faith in God's Word.

Fourteen days after receiving the first round of chemo while shampooing my hair in the shower, I noticed a clump of hair in my hand. "Oh boy, it's starting," I said to myself as more hair came out during the rinse. My doctor told me this would happen. Breast cancer survivors, whom I had the opportunity to talk to, shared their hair loss experiences. Plus, when I Googled chemotherapy and hair loss, docetaxel — a medicine in my chemotherapy regiment — was listed as one that would cause 100% hair loss. I rebuked the idea. But now, seeing the hair loss, I said, "Lord, rather than wait for my hair to all fall out, I will get it cut." So, after showering, my mom and I went to Great Clips, which was not far from home. In the past, I have worn short hairstyles, but never any style near baldness. Fortunately, I was pleased with my haircut and thought to myself, "Oh, not bad." The cut was a smooth and seamless transition to no hair. Sometime later, I noticed my nails slightly darkening, but they remained intact. I also noticed my hot flashes were nearly "*GONE!*"

People with good intentions were quick to tell me what other side effects to expect: nausea, vomiting, numbness, dry mouth, dry eye, pain, weakness, etc. My doctor prescribed medicines and suggested over-the-counter medicines to purchase in anticipation of these symptoms. While I filled the prescriptions, I prayed without ceasing and believed God would shelter me from these side effects. Well, guess what? While I experienced several symptoms such as temporary dry eye, fatigue, and a heaviness in my legs, I never took one pill! Over time, signs of the symptoms were most evident when I took Barkley for our regular walk around the subdivision. There were slight hills in the area that I did not think I would be able to walk up. Once I made it to the top, I had to sit on a bench. Isn't God good! Thank God for the bench at the top of the hill that enabled me to regain my strength.

Unlike others, I did not accept being sick. Nor did I ever considered myself as being sick. When someone said to me, "You look good." Initially, I would be offended. How did they expect me to look? Then I thought about it. I did not look like someone battling cancer. I understood that the battle with cancer was not mine but the Lord's (2 Chronicles 20:15). Therefore, I did not meet someone's expectation of being sick: extreme weight loss, withdrawn, frail, distraught, hopeless, etc. Instead, I was at peace, hopeful, joyful, and living my life with expectation. I was blessed despite the discomfort I experienced with the Neulasta shot, the loss of my breasts, hair, and weight loss due to no appetite.

A few weeks after my surgery and treatments, my insurance covered purchasing prosthetic breasts and bras from Nordstrom. Who knew that the fitting for the prosthetics would be so involved? I had to decide on the type, shape, size, and color. It also took time to decide on bra styles. Both of which I thought I would walk out the door with that day. But oh no, the prosthetics and selected bras had to be ordered. The bras had to be made with pockets for the prosthetics. This would allow me to slip the prosthetics in and out of my new bras with ease. A couple of weeks later, swinging my shopping bag in my hand, I walked out of Nordstrom with breast prosthetics and bras. I had to laugh, and in that laughter, I realized I was not troubled by the thought or sight of this act. Earlier, I mentioned I would not let my breast or hair define me, so I focused on God, His promises, and my health. "…And the peace of God, which surpasses all understanding, [guarded my] heart and mind through Christ Jesus" (Philippians 4:19).

Speaking of hair, I bought some. I got caught up at a wig shop and found three styles I thought looked pretty good on me. I wore the wigs to work. Sometimes while driving down the highway on my way home from work, I would snatch it off my head whenever a hot flash kicked in. I wore the wigs to church. I, however, could not take the hair off in church, so I wiped the beads of sweat from my face and fanned a lot in the beginning. And occasionally, when I went to other public places, I wore a wig. I recall a young lady at work, a breast cancer survivor, giving me several lightweight scarf-like headpieces to wear. I was so thankful for her kindness.

Nonetheless, I quickly tired of the headpieces and embraced my bald look publicly and privately. After putting on my makeup, I could not believe how comfortable and worry-free it was to be bald. To my surprise, I realized I was equally as comfortable without my breasts. Unfortunately, people can make you uncomfortable and remind you of what you don't have. People are accustomed to seeing women without hair but not without breasts.

Chemotherapy ended in June 2016, and my hair immediately started to grow back slowly. Two years later, Raymond and I traveled to a resort in Costa Rica, a celebratory trip after cancer. By now, I had quite a bit of hair on my head with a few noticeable changes. My sandy dark brown hair was now extremely soft, black, and curly. This was great. I did not have to worry about getting my hair wet. However, the reality of not having breasts when I donned my swimsuit made me a little self-conscious. Unlike my bras, my swimsuits did not have pockets for my prosthetic breasts, and there was no hiding my flat chest. I learned to select tops that would look best on me. Low-cut blouses and halter tops were a no-no. If a blouse had pockets for my prosthetic breasts, they would not stay secure when I bent over. They would move, leaving an apparent space between the blouse and my chest. I was not too fond of that because if I could see it, others would too. I was self-conscious of this, and it was evident to me as I interacted with people at the resort.

I usually don't hesitate to share my testimony with others, so being at the resort was no different. We met two wonderful couples with whom we socialized throughout the trip. I felt comfortable sharing my testimony with the women. We also met a group of lovely ladies whom I spoke with briefly in passing every day. I did not share my testimony with them for two reasons. First, I did not spend much time around them, so the opportunity did not present itself. And secondly, they seemed to have a puzzled look when they saw me. A puzzled look asking, why is her chest flat during the day and fuller in the evening? I decided not to hold a conversation with them about my breast cancer. Maybe it was just me. Perhaps uneasiness was creeping in, and I needed to guard against feelings that were not of God. I did not want to worry about what others thought. I focused only on God's thoughts of me.

Reconstructive surgery was not an option for me during the double mastectomy because of the third phase of my treatment — radiation. I chose to forego reconstructive surgery, temporarily. However, if I were going to have reconstructive surgery, without question, it would not be breast implants. After all the research I did on the implant procedure and discussions with women who chose to have an implant, I knew it was not for me. If I were going to do anything, it would be the DIEP Flap Breast Reconstruction. DIEP stands for Deep Inferior Epigastric Perforator. During this procedure, the surgeon would use my body fat to reconstruct my breast — new boobs and a tummy tuck all in one. After meeting with three breast surgeons, one did not think I should consider breast reconstruction at this time. He said, "your body has been through a great deal," and suggested I wait at least a year to allow my body to recover. Considering his suggestion and the body fat needed to reconstruct my breasts, I decided not to make that decision right away. I just did not think I had enough body fat to make a difference.

Moment of Clarity
I was at peace in my dance with God because I had complete faith that He would carry me through this process. I also knew if I believed I was victorious, it should be evident in my walk and talk. I could not say I was a believer — trusting, believing, and thanking God for my healing while looking hopeless, sad, and defeated. That's what the enemy wanted me to do — focus on insignificant issues instead of my God. No! Daily, I shored up my spirit by wrapping myself in God's armor that enabled me to walk the walk of faith. I knew my faith and a positive attitude would get me through this season of my life. The enemy was not going to win. As renowned Pastor Toure Roberts, founder of The Potter's House at One LA, said in his Consistency Series, "The enemy is a thief, but a thief can't steal where possession doesn't exist." I battled beautifully!

Reflection

This is a time for you to reflect on your "battle beautifully" moment(s). Journal the experience: Where were you? What were you doing? Were you prepared to respond? How did you feel? Who did you tell?

_____

_____

_____

_____

_____

_____

_____

_____

_____

_____

_____

_____

_____

_____

_____

_____

_____

_____

_____

_____

_____

_____

_____

Reflection Questions for Discussion
1. Do you understand the power and authority you have over the enemy?
2. Do you understand the purpose and power of the spiritual armor God has equipped you with? (Reference Ephesians 6:10-20)
3. Describe a situation where you confidently used God's armor. How did you feel?
4. What's your moment of clarity?

_____

_____

_____

_____

_____

_____

_____

_____

_____

_____

_____

_____

_____

_____

_____

_____

_____

_____

_____

Section Four

Rising Up with Healing in My Wings (*Restoring*)

Therefore, having these promises, beloved,
let us cleanse ourselves from all filthiness of the flesh and spirit,
perfecting holiness in the fear of God.
~ 2 Corinthians 7:1 ~

"The promises of God are meant to lead us to purity of life.
But they do not do so automatically; we have to appropriate them
and access their power by choosing to use them as God intended."[1]

Chapter 10

Fully Relying on God

And my God shall supply all [my] needs according to
His riches in glory by Christ Jesus.
~ Philippians 4:19 ~

The LORD is my strength and my shield; My heart trusted in
Him, and I am helped; Therefore, my heart greatly rejoices,
And with my song I will praise Him.
~ Psalm 28:7 ~

Do you remember the parable of the good Samaritan found in Luke 10:25-37? Jesus spoke of a traveler who had been robbed, beaten, and left for dead alongside the road. A priest passed him by, and then a Levite did the same, but a Samaritan stopped to help the traveler in his time of need. Although I was not battered and bruised by the Grace of God, I was shown much love and given much assistance. God blessed me immensely during this time and continues to bless me! I had no worries. He took care of me through the kindness of others who heeded the call!

As I began the third treatment, my employment contract at Edward Jones ended. I had no income other than unemployment. While I searched for the next job opportunity, my immediate thoughts were, how will I pay for my cancer treatment? How am I going to pay the mortgage? What about payments for health insurance? Car insurance? Utilities? etc. In Isaiah 43:26, God said, "Put Me in remembrance of My Word...." And Isaiah 55:11 says, "So shall My Word be that goes forth from My mouth; It shall not return to Me void...." During this period of unemployment, I stood on God's promises and reminded God of His Word. Lord God, you said in your Word...!

First of all, my bout with cancer was no surprise to my Heavenly

Father, and He knew this day would come. In Matthew 6:25-34, His Word says, "...Do not worry...." I did not. Instead, I praised and thanked God for His faithfulness. He exceeded my expectations.

Since I worked as a contractor, I was able to obtain healthcare insurance through the Healthcare Marketplace. It never dawned on me that my gynecologist for many years was not in my new healthcare network. I continued to get my mammogram at the usual location and did not hesitate to meet with the breast surgeon recommended by my gynecologist. Regretfully, I never checked to see if either was in the network. I, however, became acutely aware of this problem when the breast surgeon's nurse informed me that my Cigna insurance would not authorize the MRI ordered by an out-of-network physician. I initially panicked because I had breast cancer. It's official. I needed treatment. A calm came over me when the nurse shared that the doctor, from whom I had planned to get a second opinion, was in the network. The following week I met with the breast surgeon at Barnes Jewish Christian Hospital (BJC). The MRI was ordered with no problem. Look at God!

God provided two blessings. First, I was in the wrong place, and God got me to where He wanted me to be. During a follow-up visit with the initial breast surgeon, I mentioned that I had scheduled a meeting with another doctor. He thought it was good to get a second opinion. He was not at all offended. The doctor, with whom I had planned to meet with, had been recommended by a family friend's physician based in Atlanta. I thought the BJC doctor was an oncologist. I was not paying attention. It turned out the doctor was a breast surgeon. Second, when the insurance company initially denied the MRI, the doctor had the office personnel check to see if the BJC breast surgeon was in my network. Sometimes, God will put other people in your life to work for you. I was thankful that they called to confirm if the new doctor was in Cigna's network on my behalf. God orchestrated all of this! God also provided me with a third blessing. I had amassed a hefty doctor's bill because of the various procedures and tests. Additionally, I had had a mammogram and an ultrasound at a hospital that was also not in my network. Upon receiving the bill, I applied for financial assistance. One hundred percent of my expenses were covered, and I could start fresh without the previous expenses hanging over me. To this day, I sing God's praises because He was at work on my behalf. Thank you, Lord Jesus!

Scripture says, "...you do not have because you do not ask" (James 4:2). Ask in Jesus' name, be specific, and do not doubt you will receive. As I went through my treatments, I asked God for assistance with my expenses. Through conversation with others, the Holy Spirit revealed the following non-profit organizations based in St. Louis:

Gateway to Hope "provides critical support [to women with breast cancer] to reduce financial and emotional burdens empowering individuals to focus on their health." From the time of my diagnosis through the end of my treatment, Gateway to Hope - St. Louis provided funds for my health insurance and gas to travel to and from my doctors visits and treatments. They also provided a one-time mortgage payment.

Real Men Wear Pink comprises African American men from various professional backgrounds who are dedicated to "supporting women and families experiencing hardships and struggles due to the effects of breast cancer in [the] local [St. Louis] community." I was nominated for their award and was selected to receive $1,000 to assist with my expenses.

Barnes Jewish Christian Hospital provided a $500 stipend to cover my utilities, paid directly to each company. During the times I was unable to eat due to the chemo, the nutritional department had cases of Ensure delivered to my home.

The Breakfast Club is "a sisterhood of breast cancer survivors and co-survivors, reaching out to make a difference." They provided mental, spiritual, and financial support.

Empowerment Zone is a network of friends who provided a care package that included gift cards, food, and therapeutic items.

To my surprise, my friend and brother in Christ, Rev. Dr. Jeffrey Williams, stopped by with a donation collected by his congregation. The Holy Spirit also put me on the hearts and minds of many friends who came by with prepared food and financial blessings. What a blessing!

Moment of Clarity
"Every word of God is pure; He is a shield to those who put their trust in Him" (Proverbs 30:5). God's promises are true, and He is faithful. You must ask, believe, and trust Him. He will deliver!

Reflection

This is a moment for you to reflect on the time(s) you "fully relied on God." Journal the experience: What was going on with you? How did you respond? How did you feel when you realized it was nobody but God? Who did you tell?

_____

_____

_____

_____

_____

_____

_____

_____

_____

_____

_____

_____

_____

_____

_____

_____

_____

_____

_____

_____

_____

_____

_____

Reflection Questions for Discussion

1. We all have a testimony. How can you or do you share your testimony to encourage others to stand on God's promises?
2. What can you confidently say God did for you in the midst of your storm?
3. Were you patient while you waited for the manifestation of God's promise(s)? Or did you think God needed your help?
4. What's your moment of clarity?

_____

_____

_____

_____

_____

_____

_____

_____

_____

_____

_____

Chapter 11

Comforted by His Peace

You will keep him in perfect peace,
Whose mind is stayed on You, Because he trusts in You.
~ Isaiah 26:3 ~

These things I have spoken to you, that in Me you may have
peace. In the world you will have tribulation;
but be of good cheer, I have overcome the world.
~ John 16:33 ~

Preaching the Gospel landed Paul in prison and on death row. While in prison, he overcame feelings of abandonment by recognizing the presence of God. He reflected on God's faithfulness by reminding himself of God's purpose for his life (2 Timothy 4). During times of uncertainty, it is easy to focus on the situation instead of focusing on God. Of course, this is precisely what the enemy wants us to do. This allows him to plant seeds of doubt in our minds. Paul's story is an excellent reminder that God's peace comes when we focus on and trust in Him. As I prepared for radiation treatment, I was able to reflect on what God had already brought me through. Often, I recited Philippians 4:13, "I can [endure] all things through Christ who strengthens me." "Yea, though I walk through the valley of the shadow of death, I will fear no evil; For You are with me; Your rod and Your staff, they comfort me" (Psalm 23:4).

My initial visit with the radiation oncologist was nothing like my second visit. My Aunt Jean, a retired nurse, visiting from Wilson, North Carolina, accompanied me to the first visit. During this visit, the doctor talked about my treatment plan and what I could expect. I carefully listened to what was being stated. As the doctor talked, my mind wondered and I asked myself, "Why was radiation necessary? I am cancer free and no longer had breasts." I waited patiently for the doctor to finish his preliminary statements, and then I pulled out my list of questions based on my research of breast cancer and what I learned about radiation. In this exchange, I asked many questions and learned a great deal more about the disease. The doctor confirmed the findings I discussed with him, stating that, "Radiation therapy will reduce the risk of cancer reoccurring." "Okay, but my cancerous breasts have been removed, and there were no signs of disease in my lymph nodes." "Yes," he said. And went on to say, "Radiation will ensure that no cancerous cells have gotten under the collarbone or anywhere else." Through my research, I learned that radiation "destroys any remaining mutated cells in the breast or armpit area after surgery."[1] Radiation is a viable treatment, but I also found a list of short-term and long-term side effects on the internet. In addition to my research, my doctor also provided me with information. Armed with a wealth of information, I mentally prepared for phase three of the dance.

Having completed six rounds of chemo and recovered from a double mastectomy, I thought I was ready for radiation. However, discussing the treatment and going through the preparation motions was like no other. The second visit was all about radiation planning and mapping. The process began with a particular X-ray machine called a Simulator and finished in the "mold room." A soft plastic mold was made of my upper body to ensure I lay in the same position during treatment. It was important for my head, neck, arms, and torso to be in the same place to ensure the accuracy of external radiation beams. It was also essential to keep the radiation away from my heart to prevent cardiovascular problems and protect other vital organs.

All was going well until the doctor came in to mark the areas for the radiation beams. As he started to mark the areas on my chest, tears welled up in my eyes and ran down the sides of my face. I tried to be strong and mumbled, "Help me, Jesus." I still trusted Jesus. However, this was a very emotional procedure for me. I think much of my feelings had a lot to do with my thoughts about radiation. Before starting radiation, I attended a Breakfast Club meeting where I ran into a former co-worker, whom I had not seen in quite some time. As we talked, she mentioned that radiation damaged her heart. While I wanted to be aware of potential side effects, I was careful not to internalize information because the long-term effects of cancer treatment can vary. After the doctor finished, the radiology technician put clear waterproof tape over each mark to ensure I did not remove them when I showered. The tape would stay on for approximately one or two weeks. As necessary, the tape would be replaced, and my skin remarked.

My next visit was to receive the first round of 28, ten-minute, radiation treatments administered Monday through Friday. I was given specific instructions to use creams and powders on the treated area to avoid blistering and minimize skin darkening. In preparation for each visit, after showering, I would rub corn starch on the treated area. After treatment, I would cleanse the area and use a generous amount of cream to keep the treated skin area moisturized. Thankfully, I encountered no blistering. My skin did get much darker. Approximately one year after the treatments, I could still see a shadow on the left side of my chest. My skin color had not returned to normal; however, it was nearly even. Today, my skin remains dark under my left arm, and I can still see the darkened shadow from the treatment on my chest.

The beginning of my radiation process was challenging, but I found peace after the treatments began. On my first day of treatment, I checked in at the treatment center, changed into the hospital gown, and sat in the waiting room area. When the technician called my name, I followed him into the radiation room. A radio was on. As I positioned myself on the table, I asked the technicians to turn off the radio. I prepared to sing gospel music to myself. I wanted to fill my mind with thoughts of the Lord and nothing else. For ten minutes each day, I sang through the process. Fortunately, I did not have to sing alone. The technicians found the Christian station on the radio and played it during each visit. Singing brought me God's peace and kept my mind stayed on Him. He and I danced through each treatment with ease!

Moment of Clarity

This was not a pleasant experience. Nor was it painful. More than anything, envisioning myself positioned on the table with my chest exposed, hearing the roar of the X-ray machine called a Linear Accelerator, and seeing the external red beam was scary. I prayed that the beam would hit the targeted area. Although it was difficult, this experience reminded me that I could endure anything with Jesus by my side. Therefore, I would sing to keep God forefront in my mind. Focusing on God reminded me that He was so much bigger than my situation!

Reflection

This is a moment for you to reflect on the time(s) you were "comforted by God's peace." Journal the experience: Where were you? What were you doing? How did you respond? How did you feel when you realized it was nobody but God? Who did you tell?

_____

_____

_____

_____

_____

_____

_____

_____

_____

_____

_____

_____

_____

_____

_____

_____

_____

_____

_____

Reflection Questions for Discussion

1. What does it mean to be comforted by God's peace? Now what does it mean to you personally?
2. When you are at peace, do you sense God's presence? Where are you or what are you doing when you sense God's peace?
3. Do you share your testimony? Why or Why not?
4. What's your moment of clarity?

_____

_____

_____

_____

_____

_____

_____

_____

_____

_____

_____

_____

Chapter 12

My Faith File

*The Lord, who delivered me from the paw of the lion and
from the paw of the bear, He will deliver me from the hand
of this Philistine.*
~ 1 Samuel 17:37 ~

When David faced Goliath, he did not go into battle with a
defeated mindset. Instead, he reflected on the challenges God
had already brought him through. Because of his faith, he was
victorious. I am a witness and can attest to God's faithfulness. As
I danced through my journey with cancer, I was assured of God's
promises because He had already saved my life twice before! The
first miraculous event occurred when I was 15 or 16 years old.
I had obtained my driver's license, and like any teenager armed
with a license, I would volunteer to drive my family anywhere
and everywhere — anytime, day or night. One morning around 5
a.m., I dropped my mom off at the Newark International Airport
and headed back home. I was a fast driver and would usually
stay in the left lane. But this particular morning, I was driving
slower than usual, and my spirit said, "move over to the right
lane." Seconds after doing so, a car traveling the wrong way at
top speed in the left lane, barreled up the ramp as I drove down
the ramp to merge onto the highway. Had I not moved over, I
can only imagine the headline in the local newspaper, "Driver
Traveling in Wrong Direction, Hit and Killed Teen in Head-On
Collision."

The second miraculous event occurred in August 2004. Raymond
and I were on vacation in Aruba. He and I are adventure-seeking
tourists. We especially enjoy doing new things. On day two of
our vacation, we boarded a "Happy Hour Boat" for a snuba-
diving excursion. Snuba is a cross between snorkeling and scuba-
diving. The boat was going to make two stops in deep water to
allow passengers to snuba-dive in 20 or 60 feet of water. The
boat made its first stop in 60 feet of water. While a family of four

went snuba-diving, others on the boat snorkeled. The water was vividly clear with a rich deep blue color. It was beautiful. It was massive. It was intimidating.

Raymond and I, who were new to such an adventure, chose the second stop where the water was not as deep as the first stop. After two seconds of instructions, we donned our life-saving gear and went into the water. There were seven of us — the guide and six adventurers. Each oxygen cord was tethered to a single tank that floated on the water's surface, allowing each of us to travel 20 feet down. As we descended further beyond the surface, we could almost walk on the bottom of the ocean. This section of the water was not dark, nor did it appear to be as massive as I thought. It reminded me of a time in Barbados on a submarine excursion, 125 feet beneath the surface in the Atlantic Ocean, Raymond and I watched a meticulous choreography performed by beautiful fish as we peered out of the sub's small window. Now this time, we were excited to actually swim in the ocean alongside colorful fish and watch them change their formation as soon as one fish moved in a different direction. Upon descent, I noticed that Raymond had returned to the surface. The guide followed him. Raymond is a much better swimmer than I. I wondered what was going on. I later learned that Raymond was not comfortable breathing under water with the provided equipment. Fortunately, the guide talked him into rejoining the group. Thank God he did because what happened next is nothing short of a miracle.

During our two seconds of instructions, we were told how to release ear pressure during descent. To enable pressure to release from our ears — similar to what is done on an airplane — we were told to "hold [our] nose and blow." "Okay, I got it," I said to myself. Following the instructions, I had received, I descended into the water. I held my nose and blew. I could see that the water and fish were amazingly beautiful. I, however, held my nose and blew one time too many or too hard and I accidentally blew the mouthpiece out of my mouth. I was afraid to open my mouth to reinsert the mouthpiece. Suddenly, the water that had been so clear was now cloudy. I gave the distress signal, but when I looked around, I could not see anyone. I remember telling myself not to panic, but I needed to get to the surface. I tried to remove the ten-pound belt from my waist, but to no avail. I did not panic, I started to swim upward and that's all I remember until I reached the surface of the water and gasped for air. I later learned that while I did not see anyone, Raymond saw me. He and the guide came to my aid. I literally don't recall anything after attempting to swim to the top. I believe I passed out, and my guardian angel breathed for me. I never saw or felt Raymond's touch or the guide helping me swim to the top. It's by God's grace that I am here today.

Throughout my cancer treatment dance, I often reminded myself of these miraculous instances of God's deliverance. Just as God was with David; He was with me. As a result, I could face my "Goliath" of cancer with the utmost confidence that I was safe in the arms of the Almighty God!

As I write this book, I have two testimonies to add to my faith file. On Friday, Nov. 8, 2019, after checking on my neighbor and walking back to my house, I fell at the base of my driveway. A last minute decision to check the mailbox before continuing my walk up the driveway, I turned too quickly and fell. Once inside, I began to feel and notice my hand swelling and quickly turning black and blue. I rushed to the nearby Urgent Care facility. The x-ray of my left hand revealed two fractures — my index finger and ring finger. Additional x-rays and a CT scan showed no other breaks. Fortunately, I experienced no pain or visible bruises anywhere other than my hand. The ring finger, however, warranted further inspection by an orthopedic surgeon.

The surgeon confirmed the fracture in the ring finger and indicated that my index finger had experienced a volar plate injury — comparable to a strained ligament that bent back too far. Surgery was not necessary. I only needed a splint and four to six weeks to heal.

As I shared my testimony with family, friends, and my Bible

study sisters in Christ, I thanked God for cushioning my fall. I realized my fall could have been much worse as my driveway is on an incline. I thanked God that it was my left hand and not my right hand. I thanked God that there were no other broken bones. Even though I filled the pain medication prescriptions, I never had to take one. Lastly, I thanked God for allowing me to be a one-handed typist — which allowed me to share my testimony with you. God is good, and His mercy is everlasting.

My second testimony occurred in 2020 during the COVID-19 quarantine. Fear, a spirit not of God, invaded my spirit. I don't know where it came from. Yes, I do. It came from the enemy. I don't know why I was experiencing it. On second thought, yes, I do. Again, it was the enemy, whose sole mission is "to steal, to kill, and to destroy" (John 10:10). Even though I had not watched much news about the pandemic, apparently, I watched enough because it took an emotional toll on me. At night, I became nervous. I could not sleep for fear of not waking up. Occasionally, I had chills, but never a fever. I was constantly checking my temperature. I cannot tell you how many times I almost went to the emergency room in the middle of the night. I now understand the statement, "The battle starts in the mind." The enemy looked for a window of opportunity to plant a negative seed in my mind. I guess I provided the opportunity when a nurse practitioner asked if I had noticed any changes in my breast area while performing my monthly breast exams. She wanted to make sure I had no problems or concerns as appointments were being rescheduled eight to ten weeks out due to COVID-19.

Until that moment, I had no concerns. A day or so later, I felt a slight discomfort in an area on the left side under my breast area. I attributed it to working in the yard. Days later, the discomfort continued. Of course, that was all I needed to allow my thoughts to take flight. Proverbs 23:7 says, "For as he thinks in his heart, so *is* he…." I Googled COVID-19 symptoms and compared them to symptoms for pneumonia. I noticed that my mouth was dry, causing me to drink several gallons of water throughout the day and night. I prayed and asked God what was going on? Why am I experiencing this? The Holy Spirit placed in my spirit to Google, dry mouth. I Googled the question, "What causes dry mouth?" The information indicated that chemotherapy, HIV, and diabetes could cause dry mouth. Well, neither applied to me but the next sentence did – "Stress, anxiety, and nervousness could also cause dry mouth." I was experiencing anxiety attacks. Once I identified the cause of my concerns, I suited up for the fight and was *victorious* over my fears through God's Word, the name of Jesus and His blood!

"Each of us will face fear at some point; it is what we do with it that matters most. We must claim our position as God's children. We have the power to overcome fear when we apply His Word to our lives."[1] I prayed. Sometimes I cried. I asked others to pray and stand in agreement with me because Matthew 18:19 says, "… if two of you agree on earth concerning anything that they ask, it will be done for them by My Father in heaven." As I turned this battle over to God, I gained a better understanding of Matthew 18:18 which says, "whatever you bind on earth will be bound in heaven, and whatever you loose on earth will be loosed in heaven." Standing in God's truth, I bound "the fiery darts [fear and anxiety] of the adversary" and loosed God's calm and peace. I became "spiritually alert" and recognized when an attack of the enemy was trying to rear its ugly head. Each day I put on the whole armor of God to fight against the enemy's traps. In His word, God said, "And I give them eternal life, and they shall never perish; neither shall anyone snatch them out of My hand" (John 10:28).

Moment of Clarity
God watches over us and protects us from seen and unseen dangers. All we have to do is look over our lives to see what God has brought us through. Trust and believe Him. We can speak God's promises over our lives. Faith, however, is put into action when we stand on His Word and believe it to be true. Therefore, I knew I would be victorious in this battle with cancer! With every trial and tribulation, I thanked God for keeping His righteous right hand on me, and His loving arms around me. My God

moments are my testimonies to glorify Him and edify the body for His purposes. All of the glory belongs to Him!

Reflection

This is a moment for you to reflect on your "faith file." Journal your experience(s): Where were you? What were you doing? How did you respond? How did you feel when you realized it was nobody but God? Who did you tell?

_____

_____

_____

_____

_____

_____

_____

_____

_____

_____

_____

_____

_____

_____

_____

_____

_____

_____

_____
_____
_____
_____
_____
_____
_____
_____
_____
_____
_____
_____
_____
_____
_____
_____
_____
_____
_____
_____
_____
_____
_____
_____
_____
_____
_____

_____

_____

_____

_____

_____

_____

_____

_____

_____

_____

_____

_____

_____

_____

_____

Reflection Questions for Discussion

1. Do you have a "faith file?" If yes, what does a "faith file" mean to you? If not, what are you waiting for?
2. When the storms of life happen, do you reflect on what God has already done for you? How does that make you feel? Does it boost your confidence?
3. Who have you encouraged to maintain a "faith file?"
4. What's your moment of clarity?

_____

_____

_____

_____

_____

_____

_____

_____
_____
_____
_____
_____
_____
_____
_____
_____
_____
_____
_____
_____
_____
_____
_____
_____
_____
_____
_____
_____
_____
_____
_____
_____
_____
_____

Section Five

Gliding Before the Lord with All My Might
(Rejoicing)

*But now, thus says the LORD, who created you, O Jacob, And He
who formed you, O Israel: "Fear not, for I have redeemed you;
I have called you by your name; You are Mine. When you pass
through the waters, I will be with you; And through the rivers,
they shall not overflow you. When you walk through the fire, you
shall not be burned, Nor shall the flame scorch you.
~ Isaiah 43:1 ~*

*Every word of God is pure; He is a shield to those
who put their trust in Him.
~ Proverbs 30:5 ~*

Chapter 13

Praise Report

Rejoice always, pray continually, give thanks in all circumstances;
for this is God's will for you in Christ Jesus.
~ 1 Thessalonians 5:16-18 ~

There's a story in the Bible about ten men who Jesus cleansed of leprosy (Luke 17:11-19). Of the ten, only one glorified God. When the one came back, Jesus said, "Were there not ten cleansed? But where are the nine" (v.17)? The ten men were quick to beg Jesus to heal them, saying, "Master, have mercy on us" (v.13)! Yet only one of the ten shared his testimony and thought it was important to thank God for his healing. I don't know about you, but I want to be amongst the ten percent who gave God praise. This is precisely why I cannot keep quiet when I think about what God has brought me through. I want to be obedient to what He has tasked me to do. Psalm 150:6 says, "Let everything that has breath praise the LORD. Praise the LORD!"

I have praised God through every step, twist, turn, and dip in my dance. In the beginning, I called to share praise reports following my doctors' appointments. My first written praise report followed my second round of chemo. From February through September of 2016, after appointments, surgeries, and treatments, I sent out praise reports. I sent them to the shepherd of my church, Bishop Jones, my family members, and friends. I had to praise God for His grace and mercy. Praising God was necessary to do for two reasons. First, it strengthened my trust and faith in God as I witnessed Him moving in my life. Second, I witnessed God's faithfulness during this dance. When God blesses us, and we are thankful for the blessing, guess what? He will bless us again, and again, and again. I did not want to miss my blessings. I had to glorify the Father, not only because of His blessings to me, but because of who He is.

As always, I met with my oncologist before treatments. During the visit just before round two of chemo, he said, "The tumors are responding well to the chemo, and they are no longer present." I said, "Praise God. Thank you, Jesus! We're done. No need for further treatment." "Not so fast," he said. "You will need to continue the schedule of treatments to make sure this is a long-term response. Therefore, you will need to complete all six rounds of chemotherapy." Of course, I Googled what he shared. I learned that newly diagnosed patients must continue taking their prescribed treatments to ensure a "complete response" that no cancer is present in the body. Stopping the treatments would be premature. Out went a praise report!

On Friday, June 17, 2016, I texted a praise report that announced the completion of chemotherapy. A picture of me ringing the bell accompanied the text. Ringing the bell was significant because it alerts everyone in the Siteman Cancer Center and those in the waiting area that a patient has just completed their last round of chemo. It was a joyous moment to finally ring that bell! I thanked God for that moment. It was a double thank you because upon meeting with the oncologist, I learned that my platelet count was low based on my blood test. I understood that this is a dangerous side effect of chemotherapy because it can cause blood loss and damage to internal organs. Of course, I was concerned and disappointed. The thought of not completing my sixth treatment or having a blood transfusion to proceed with chemotherapy was the last thing I wanted to address. I tried not to worry. I, however, was concerned. All I could do was wait for a decision, and while doing so, I said a quick prayer. "I love the LORD, for He heard my voice; He heard my cry for mercy" (Psalm 116:1, (NIV). God answered my prayer! I was able to proceed!

After ringing the bell, I mentally prepared myself for a double mastectomy. I was so thankful that I did not develop chemotherapy-induced peripheral neuropathy (CIPN). CIPN is a potential side effect of chemotherapy — such as damaged nerves and the loss of feeling in arms, hands, and feet. Based on what I had read, doctors don't know why some patients experience neuropathy and others don't. A childhood friend, whom I later learned was a breast cancer survivor, experienced extreme swelling in both arms and hands and had no movement in either after chemo. Praise God for her. After some time, the swelling went away in one arm and hand, and the feeling returned. Unfortunately, however, not so much in the other. To minimize my chances, my breast surgeon suggested I always use my right arm for future tests (lab work, blood pressure checks, IVs, etc.) since the tumors were on the left, and chemotherapy was directed to that area.

Armed with this information, I always offer my right arm for any medical procedure. On the day of my surgery, the nurse prepping me asked for my left arm to insert the needle for the IV. I asked him to use the right arm instead. He said the paperwork stated the left arm. I shared with him what my breast surgeon told me and requested he consult with her. He did, and the right arm it was. I share this information because, often, we accept what the professional says. I implore everyone to be proactive in any medical treatment or procedure. I have met too many women who could not tell me about their breast cancer diagnosis —type or stage— only that the treatment was for breast cancer. I get it. Some people don't want to know. I, however, encourage people to learn and ask questions. This was one of the things my doctors appreciated about me. I did my research and came prepared with questions. The surgery was a success. Out went another praise report!

Throughout my dance, I was pretty good at mentally preparing myself for what was to come. However, I did not expect a second surgery to remove the port. My breast surgeon removed and tested the first row of lymph nodes under my arm. To ensure the absence of cancer, my oncologist wanted to wait for my lab results before removing the port. Once the results were in, surgery was scheduled. The port would be removed after I had recovered from breast surgery and before radiation treatments began. It made sense. Praise God, that's another praise report!

After an overnight stay in the hospital, I departed with new gear that became a part of my attire for two weeks — a drainage tube that extended from the surgical incision in the breast area with a sack to catch the fluid — one on each side. The drainage tube, designed to remove the blood and fluid buildup, was necessary to reduce swelling and eliminate the chance of infection. As the sacks filled, I had to pour the fluid into a measuring cup and log the fluid levels with dates and times. After about day four, the liquid color lightened, and with each passing day, I noticed a decrease in the fluid levels. This process was essential to continue until no fluid was present. At the end of two weeks, there was no drainage, and the tubes were removed during a visit to the doctor's office. The nurse practitioner literally pulled them out. It was not painful, just a weird feeling and sight to see. I could not believe the length of the tubes. When the nurse practitioner removed the tubes, out went another praise report! A praise report also followed the completion of radiation! I continue to give verbal praise reports to family and friends following my yearly CT scans. In 2021, I reached my five-year mark of being cancer-free!

Moment of Clarity
The trials and tribulations we face can be scary, but God is a healer, provider, way maker, deliverer, protector, and so much more. "No temptation has overtaken you except such as is common to [humankind]; but God *is* faithful, who will not allow you to be tempted beyond what you are able, but with the temptation will also make the way of escape, that you may be able to bear *it*" (1 Corinthians 10:13). This scripture tells me that anything God allows me to go through, He will bring me through it. For this blessing, as Tasha Cobbs Leonard says in the title of her song, "Put a Praise on It," that is exactly what I did! Do not hesitate to thank God and share the good news. No rock will cry out for me (Luke 19:40)!

This is a moment for you to reflect on your "praise report." Journal your experience(s): What is your praise? Where were you? What were you doing? How did you respond? How did you feel when you realized it was nobody but God? Who did you tell?

_____

_____

_____

_____

_____

_____

_____

_____

_____

_____

_____

_____

_____

_____

_____

_____

_____

_____

_____

_____

Reflection Questions for Discussion
1. What has God brought you through? Was it a coincident or God orchestrated? How do you know?
2. Do you consider your praise a testimony worthy of sharing?
3. Do you believe your testimony can help someone else? Why or why not? What's your moment of clarity?

_____

_____

_____

_____

_____

_____

_____

_____

_____

_____

_____

_____

_____

_____

_____

_____

_____

_____

_____

_____

_____

_____

Chapter 14

In the Morning

...Weeping may endure for a night, But joy comes in the morning.
~ Psalm 30:5 ~

At an early age, I heard my grandma and other adults say, "If I didn't have a problem, I wouldn't know God could solve it." I had no clue what it meant. Today, I do. No one wants to experience hard times, pain, suffering, disappointment, self-doubt, financial woes, job loss, a health scare, or any of life's frustrations. We all want to victoriously dance through life without a care in the world, worry-free. Yet, God's Word tells us in John 16:33, "...In the world, you shall have tribulations; but be of good cheer, I have overcome the world." James 1:2-3 says, "My brethren, count it all joy when you fall into various trials, knowing that the testing of your faith produces patience." If we had a problem-free life or could solve our problems in this fallen world, we would think we were in control and have no need for a Savior.

Trials and tribulations remind us just how much we need Jesus. As I reflect on my dance through breast cancer and think about other challenges I have faced, I know Jesus was with me. This is why Marvin Sapp's song, "Never Would Have Made It," rings true in my life. I have grown in my faith, and I am more aware of God's presence in my life. I am learning to see Jesus in everything. When I read a daily devotional, sing a song of praise, hear a sermon, or have a conversation, I know God is speaking to me. I cannot help but wonder about the message or the lesson and how it applies to me.

On the morning of December 22, 2019, I completed reading a six-part daily devotional series published in *The Word for You Today* by Debby and Bob Gass, titled, "How to Win Life's Battles."[1] The dos and don'ts of the series resonated with me. Each day during my reading, I was able to think about my actions during my dance. I personalized this chapter with keywords based on the steps outlined within the devotional that applied to my walk. The beauty of this reading is that these steps apply to any situation and can help us conquer any challenge, big or small. Trials and tribulations are a fact of life, so the question is, What's the approach going to be to rise victoriously?

The authors of this six-part series used the victory of King Jehoshaphat to teach us "how to win life's battles" (2 Chronicles 20): The *first* line of defense is to *"identify the enemy."* The author says, "Many times, the enemy is our attitude! It's not so much what's happening that gets us down. It's our response to the situation."[1] The battle starts in the mind. "Don't see a problem, panic, and be consumed with fear and ask, 'Why me, Lord?' Instead, fear should motivate believers to conquer the problem and draw closer to God."[2]

The evening I experienced my "it" — tribulation — began in February 2016 with a breast cancer diagnosis. I had no idea how I would manage through my trial, but God knew. Standing on His Word, I claimed victory. My morning — victory — came at the end of September 2016 with the last radiation treatment. As I reflect on my dance, I realized I had not emphasized "cancer." I emphasized God and His promises, and because of this, I grew spiritually and walked victoriously.

My Key Words: Conviction and Expectation
Following the first ultrasound, the nurse's face showed fear and great concern, but God's Word says, "Yet in all things we are more than conquerors through Him who loved us" (Romans 8:37). "To be more than conquerors mean we face the trials of life with the certainty that we are not alone. We have a mighty Father who fights for us. We approach the darkest valleys with confidence, knowing that nothing can happen to us that is not permitted by our loving Father for our good" (Psalm 23:4; Romans 8:28).[3] I knew God was with me, and I knew I was going to be okay. I recognized this dance as a process that I expected to come through victoriously!

Second, "admit your own inadequacy." "The only people God can't help are those who don't think they need His help."[4] Chris Tiegreen says, "If you fight in your own strength, you'll lose. But when you draw on the power of God's Spirit that's within you, you'll win."[5] Often when a problem arises, or a situation occurs, I try to figure it out or work it out myself — and the outcome is not always favorable. I then call on God to clean up my mess. When the doctor shared the biopsy results, without question, I knew this situation was bigger than me. I called on God. "Cursed is the man who trusts in man and makes flesh his strength..." (Jeremiah 17:5). "Blessed is the man who trusts in the Lord, and whose hope is the Lord" (v7).

My Key Word: Dependency

A dear friend of mine wanted me to take a holistic approach to treatment rather than chemotherapy to treat the cancer in my body. While I appreciated her suggestion and concern, I thought about Isaiah 45:2, which says, "I will go before you and make the crooked places straight." God had already moved me from one hospital and doctor's care and placed me in the care of another hospital and doctor. I was not going to step out on my own. I kept my hope in God because I believed He placed me where He wanted me to be.

Third, "take your problems to the Lord." When you are facing life's battles, prayer should be your first resort, not your last. In the past, I never thought first to take my concerns to God. Yet His Word says, "Cast your burden on the LORD, and He shall sustain you; He shall never permit the righteous to be moved" (Psalm 55:22). Yeah, I thought, but some things are so small, I can handle it. I will bother God with the big stuff. Wrong. 1 Peter 5:7 says, "Cast all your care upon Him, for He cares for you."

My Key Word: Reliance

In Charles Stanley's devotional message, *"Clinging to God's Promises,"* opens with "The Bible is a gold mine of promises for believers."[6] If you Google the number of promises in the Bible, some searches show more than 3000 promises, and others more than 5000. While I don't know them all, I was able to speak with conviction because I believed the promise for my healing to be true. "But He *was* wounded for our transgressions, He *was* bruised for our iniquities; The chastisement for our peace *was* upon Him, And by His stripes we *are* healed" (Isaiah 53:5). My diagnosis did not frighten me. My confidence in His Word did not waiver. I never doubted for a moment that God would not see me through the "it."

Fourth, "learn to relax in faith." Second Chronicles 20:15 clearly states, "The battle is not yours, but God's." The authors reminded me that "We don't hold God up — He holds us up! We don't have Him in our hands. He has us in His hands!"[7] Nothing that happens to us catches God by surprise. In His Word, He said He goes before us. He does not need our help. Actually, He tells us in Isaiah 41:10 that He will strengthen us and help us; "I will uphold you with My righteous right hand." We don't need to interfere. When we do, we can delay our blessing — our joy that comes in the "morning."

My Key Words: Trust and Believe
God is faithful… "For I know the plans I have for you, declares the LORD, plans to prosper you and not to harm you, plans to give you hope and a future" (Jeremiah 29:11). I was courageous because I knew He was with me through each test, each round of chemo, every surgery, and each radiation treatment.

Fifth, "stand firm." This act of standing firm is "a mental attitude of quiet confidence that says, 'I'm going to trust God.'"[8] I'm going to "stand firm on God's character. Stand firm on [God's Word]"[9]— His truth. Trust that God will do what He says He will do.

My Key Word: Attitude
I had a made-up mind. I was going to trust God for my healing. When the biopsy results showed pre-cancer in the right breast, I was grateful and thanked God for revealing it. As children of God, we must protect our hearts and our minds. "…Those things

which proceed out of the mouth come from the heart, and they defile a man" (Matthew 15:18). "Self-perception deceives us. We get discouraged, think negatively, become pessimists, and wonder if our faith is worth the trouble. The darkness of the world, the distortions of our flesh, and the schemes of the evil one combine to create illusions of despair. Resist them all. God's truth is remarkably contrary to what our souls perceive."[10]

Sixth and lastly, "*thank God in advance.*" When we realize how big our God is and how small our problem is, the authors affirm, "1) Your atmosphere changes. You no longer feel afraid because you have the assurance of God's presence. 2) Your attitude changes. You say, 'Lord, this may be too big for me, but it's not for You.' 3) Your approach changes. Instead of speaking words of doubt, you start speaking words of faith. Your faith honors God [and God honors your faith]."[11]

My Key Words: Gratefulness (a feeling) and Thankfulness (an act)
During my dance, I was not afraid. I was pretty surprised at how at peace I was with everything. My relationship with God had grown. Scripture says, "Trust in the Lord with all your heart, and lean not on your own understanding" (Proverbs 3:5); "…and the peace of God, which surpasses all understanding, will guard your hearts and minds through Christ Jesus" (Philippians 4:7). I put my trust in God and gave my "it" to Him. I relaxed, knowing that He had already "perfected those things that concerned me" (Psalm 138:8). I was grateful for my dance because I realized the dance was not about me. Family and friends around me danced with God as well. For example, my mother's spiritual walk strengthened. Daily, she spends time in God's Word, and we often discuss the readings together. Members of my Bible study group often reference the change witnessed in me and its impact on them.

Moment of Clarity
On Sunday, December 22, 2019, Bishop Jones preached a sermon

titled, "A Name for Every Need." It confirmed and reminded me that Jesus' name is "…Wonderful, Counselor, Mighty God, Everlasting Father, Prince of Peace" (Isaiah 9:6). Jesus talks with us, and He gives us rest. When we need a word, He gives us His Word. He has mastered every difficulty that we face. And He gives peace during the storm. We must call on Him and trust Him.

The opening scripture in this chapter is a reminder that everything has a beginning and an ending. Trials and tribulations are a part of life while we are on this side of Heaven. The night is the situation. While we are going through "it," know that God is with us. Focus on Him. Grow in the process. The morning, no matter the result, comes because "trouble don't last always!"

Reflection

This is a moment for you to reflect on your "mornings." Journal your experience(s): Describe your "it". Where were you? What were you doing? How did you respond? How did you feel? Who did you tell?

_____

_____

_____

_____

_____

_____

_____

_____

_____

_____

_____

Chapter 14 ~ In the Morning

Reflection Questions for Discussion

1. Detail your midnight? Were you overwhelmed? Did you call out the name "Jesus" for help? Did you ask the Holy Spirit to guide you?
2. What steps have you taken in the midst of the "it" storm?
3. Did you find the steps outlined in this chapter helpful?
4. What's your moment of clarity?

_____

_____

_____

_____

_____

_____

_____

_____

_____

_____

_____

_____

_____

_____

_____

_____

_____

_____

_____

_____

_____

_____

_____

_____

_____

_____

Chapter 14 ~ In the Morning

_____

_____

_____

_____

_____

_____

_____

_____

_____

_____

_____

_____

_____

_____

_____

_____

_____

_____

_____

_____

_____

_____

_____

_____

_____

_____

_____

_____

Chapter 15

Blessing to Be Used by God

"For I know the plans I have for you," declares the LORD,
"plans to prosper you and not to harm you,
plans to give you hope and a future."
~ Jeremiah 29:11(NIV) ~

I read an article posted on Bible.org that made me chuckle. It was entitled, *"The People God Uses* (Lesson 89)" by Steven J. Cole. I chuckled because it gave me flashbacks to my days as president of the National Black MBA Association, St. Louis Chapter. I see chapter board members seated around an oblong table planning and discussing strategies to implement new programs and identify qualified individuals based on background, experience, and influence to execute plans. Similar to what's suggested in the article. I imagined Jesus saying, it doesn't take all that. In the article, Cole talked about the unlikely characters Jesus chose to launch His movement — "the Church."

Had he been around, he states, "I would have advised Him to do things differently!"[1] He says he would have asked, "What were You thinking when You came up with these men to launch this movement?"[2] He said Jesus needed well-educated men — men who attended prestigious universities — scholarly men. Men who had experience with this sort of thing — a proven "track record of impressive results in the ministry."[3] Furthermore, he went on to say, "You need men of influence who have connections with important wealthy, powerful people. They need to know how to network with movers and shakers."[4] I say that's a project within a project. Paul writes in 2 Corinthians 4:7, "But we have this treasure in earthen vessels, that the excellence of the power may be of God and not of us." God gets the glory! Not man. God used ordinary people — everyday, flawed folk — for His glory!

127

The Lord declares, "For my thoughts are not your thoughts, and your ways are not my ways" (Isaiah 55:8). God sees the hearts of people! You never know when or how He will use you but know that He can and will use you for His purposes and glory! Surprise!

God surprised me with an assignment the morning of my first round of chemotherapy. I was overwhelmed and joyful at the same time. I couldn't believe it. As I sit and write the last chapter of this book, I searched my electronic "Faith File" stored in the hard drive of my mind and heart. I see how God orchestrated my life, particularly starting with my desire to write a book 20 years ago. As I mentioned initially, I wanted to write a book that would impact you and add value to your life, my reader. My testimony, by the grace of God, will bless me and benefit you. Years ago, my mom asked if I would recognize God's voice if He talked to me. Now I can say, Yes! I clearly heard Him when He planted the seed for this book. I now understand the statement, "God is working behind the scenes on your behalf." The time had not yet come for me to write a book.

God knew triple-negative breast cancer was before me, and He groomed and spiritually equipped me for the fight. And in the process, He used me to write this book and minister to others going through breast cancer. The beauty in all of this is that the book is not just for His children with breast cancer. It applies to all His children facing a trial or tribulation — their "it." Trials and tribulations are designed to show us our character and build our faith, not harm us. It's hard to believe this without experiencing God and developing a relationship with the Father. But it's true! As you read the many biblical stories in the Bible, you will quickly notice that the men and women of the Bible faced unthinkable challenges as they went through their "it." They kept the faith and came through their "it" victoriously. Take a look at Job's story. He lost everything, but for his light affliction, God abundantly restored his fortunes.

Look at Joseph. He was sold into slavery and imprisoned, yet he remained faithful to God. Because of his faithfulness, he was rewarded with the birthright in Israel and received a high position in the king's palace. Refusing to bow to the king's statue, Shadrach, Meshach, and Abednego were thrown into the fiery furnace and emerged victoriously. Why? Because Jesus was with them in the fire. This is a great visual of Christ being with you in your trial. You are never alone. What the enemy meant for evil, God will turn it around for your good. We don't know how, but we know He will. God said in His Word, "I will never leave you nor forsake you" (Hebrews 13:5). Now that alone is a shouting moment!

God spoke to me again during round three of chemotherapy when He instructed me to pray with a stranger at the Siteman Cancer Center. Surprise, again! During my trial, He did not allow me to focus on myself. He had me focus on another of His children. I've learned that God, through the Holy Spirit, communicates with us every day. In His Word, He tells us how to live our lives and demonstrates what righteous living looks like through the examples of Jesus. Through the common and flawed characters of the Bible, God shows us how to live and how not to live.

Moment of Clarity

David said in Psalm 119:71, "It is good for me that I have been afflicted, that I may learn Your statutes." There is nothing pleasant about experiencing trials and tribulations, which is why no one wants to go through "it." But think about this, if tough times are a catalyst to shape and form one's character and strengthen one's faith, how could we know what God can do for us without the "its" we experience and go through – *through* – being the operative word. During a morning walk through my subdivision, I listened to an inspirational message on YouTube entitled "Positioned to Be Blessed." The unknown speaker put things in perspective for me, which clarified my grandmother's statement, "If I didn't have a problem, I wouldn't know God could solve "it." The speaker basically said, "If you never had a health crisis, how would you know that God is a healer and by His stripes, you are healed? If you never had a financial hardship, how would you know that God is a provider?"[5] Adding to this, if door after door is closed to you, how would you know that God is a way maker? "What He opens no one can shut, and what he shuts no one can open" (Revelations 3:7 (NIV)). Do you get the point? Count it all joy. It's a blessing to be used by God!

My Prayer…

All Mighty God, creator of all things. You are all-knowing and knew that this day would come. Thank you for the privilege to approach Your throne of grace on behalf of the readers of this book. Bless them Father. Open their heart and mind so that they will come to know You as their creator, redeemer, protector, restorer, provider, healer, and most importantly, Jesus is their Lord and Savior. Strengthen their relationship with you. Create in them a "clean heart and a steadfast spirit." Forgive them for past and present sins. Help them to know and see that You are a forgiving Father. Help them to know and see that Your Word is true and pure. Help them to understand that You are "a shield to those who put their trust in [You]." Please help them to know that although the enemy may form a weapon against them, it will not prosper. As they go through a valley, their "it," let them know that You are with them. And may they forever glorify Your name. Amen, in the name of Jesus Christ, Lord and Savior!

Know that our God is bigger than your circumstance — your "it." Be ready to be used by God! It's a blessing!

This is a moment for you to reflect on your "blessings in the midst of your trial." Journal your experience(s): What is your praise? Where were you? What were you doing? How did you respond? How did you feel when you realized it was nobody but God? Who did you tell?

Reflection Questions for Discussion
1. Is it difficult for you to see your "it" as a blessing? Why?
2. When you look back at your valley experience(s), can you now see how God orchestrated your victory?
3. What is your advice, based on scripture, to someone going through their "it?"
4. What's your moment of clarity?

_____

_____

_____

_____

_____

_____

_____

_____

_____

_____

_____

_____

_____

_____

_____

_____

_____

_____

_____

_____

Epilogue

He Will Never

Psalm 9:1-10 reminds us that "God never forsakes a man or woman who places his or her trust in Him. He may allow them to wade through some very deep and cold waters, but He will never abandon them. When everyone else flees, He remains."[1] Praise Him always and give thanks!

Psalm 9:1-10
I will praise you, O Lord, with my whole heart;
I will tell of Your marvelous works.
I will be glad and rejoice in You.
I will sing praise to Your name, O Most High.
When my enemies turn back,
They shall fall and perish at Your presence.
For You have maintained my right and my cause;
You sat on the throne judging in righteousness.
You have rebuked the nations,
You have destroyed the wicked;
You have blotted out their name forever and ever
O enemy, destructions are finished forever!
And You have destroyed cities;
Even their memory has perished.
But the Lord shall endure forever;
He has prepared His throne for judgement.
He shall judge the world in righteousness;
And He shall administer judgment for the peoples
in uprightness.
The Lord also will be a refuge for the oppressed.
A refuge in times of trouble.
And those who know Your name will put their trust in You;
For You, Lord, have not forsaken those who seek You.

CONFESSION OF FAITH REFERENCE SCRIPTURES

Psalms 27

Mark 16:17

John 14:12-14

Isaiah 54:17

Colossians 1:13

1 John 4:4

Matthew 16:19

Favorite Scriptures

Spending time in God's Word is a daily reminder of His presence and His faithfulness. Focus on God and His promises, not your situation. He will see you through.

Fear not, for I *am* with you; Be not dismayed, for I *am* your God. I will strengthen you, Yes, I will help you, I will uphold you with My righteous right hand. ~ *Isaiah 41:10*

The LORD *is* near to all who call upon Him, To all who call upon Him in truth. ~ *Psalm 145:18*

Trust in the Lord with all your heart, And lean not on your own understanding; In all your ways acknowledge Him, And He shall direct your paths. ~ *Proverbs 3:5-6*

He who dwells in the secret place of the Most High Shall abide under the shadow of the Almighty. ~ *Psalm 91:10*

The Lord *is* my light and my salvation; Whom shall I fear? The Lord *is* the strength of my life; Of whom shall I be afraid? ~ *Psalm 27:1*

For by grace you have been saved through faith, and that not of yourselves; *it is* the gift of God, not of works, lest anyone should boast. ~ *Ephesians 2:8-9*

Blessed is the one who endures trials, because when he has stood the test he will receive the crown of life that God has promised to those who love him. ~ *James 1:12*

Favorite Scriptures continued

Because of the LORD's faithful love we do not perish, for His mercies never end. They are new every morning; great is your faithfulness. ~ *Lamentations 3:22-23*

Therefore we do not give up. Even though our outward person is being destroyed, our inner person is being renewed day by day. ~ *2 Corinthians 4:16*

Be strong and of good courage, do not fear nor be afraid of them; for the LORD your God, He *is* the One who goes with you. He will not leave you nor forsake you. ~ *Deuteronomy 31:6*

And the Lord will deliver me from every evil work and preserve *me* for His heavenly kingdom. To Him *be* glory forever and ever. Amen! ~ *2 Timothy 4:18*

Your word *is* a lamp to my feet, and a light to my path.
~ *Psalm 119:105*

For I know the plans I have for you, declares the LORD, plans to prosper you and not to harm you, plans to give you hope and a future. ~ *Jeremiah 29:11*

Blessed *be* the Lord, *Who* daily loads us *with benefits,* The God of our salvation! ~ *Psalm 68:19*

Blessed *are* the people who know the joyful sound! They walk, O LORD, in the light of Your countenance. ~ *Psalm 89:15*

The LORD *is* my strength and song, And He has become my salvation; He *is* my God, and I will praise Him; My father's God, and I will exalt Him. ~ *Exodus 15:2*

Favorite Scriptures continued

Then Jesus spoke to them again, saying, "I am the light of the world. He who follows Me shall not walk in darkness, but have the light of life." ~ *John 8:12*

...being confident of this very thing, that He who has begun a good work in you will complete *it* until the day of Jesus Christ... ~ Philippians 1:6

Every word of God *is* pure; He *is* a shield to those who put their trust in Him. ~ Proverbs 30:5

Finally, brethren, whatever things are true, whatever things *are* noble, whatever things *are* just, whatever things *are* pure, whatever things *are* lovely, whatever things *are* of good report, if *there is* any virtue and if *there is* anything praiseworthy—meditate on these things. ~ Philippians 4:8

And the prayer of faith will save the sick, and the Lord will raise him up. And if he has committed sins, he will be forgiven. ~ James 5:15

Now may the God of hope fill you with all joy and peace in believing, that you may abound in hope by the power of the Holy Spirit. ~ Romans 15:13

For God has not given us a spirit of fear, but of power and of love and of a sound mind. ~ *2 Timothy 1:7*

Let us hold fast the confession of *our* hope without wavering, for He who promised *is* faithful. ~ *Hebrews 10:23*

Favorite Scriptures continued

And we know that all things work together for good to those who love God, to those who are the called according to *His* purpose. *~ Romans 8:28*

And the LORD, He *is* the One who goes before you. He will be with you, He will not leave you nor forsake you; do not fear nor be dismayed. *~ Deuteronomy 31:8*

But seek first the kingdom of God and His righteousness, and all these things shall be added to you. *~ Matthew 6:33*

Delight thyself also in the LORD; and he shall give thee the desires of thine heart. *~ Psalm 37:4*

Favorite Songs

Praise God for His Word and Providence
Praise the Lord!
For it is good to sing praises to our God;
For it is pleasant, and praise is beautiful.
~ Psalm 147:1 ~

I'm Gonna Be Ready - Yolanda Adams
The Battle Is Not Yours - Yolanda Adams

More than Anything - Lamar Campbell

I Just Want to Praise You - Maurette Brown Clark

Like the Dew - Judith Christie-McAllister

He Knows My Name - Tasha Cobbs Leonard
Gracefully Broken - Tasha Cobbs Leonard
I'm Gonna Put a Praise On It - Tasha Cobbs Leonard

Bread of Heaven - Fred Hammond
God Is - Fred Hammond

God's Got a Blessing - Norman Hutchins
Encourage Yourself - Donald Lawrence
I am Healed - Donald Lawrence

God Provides - Tamela Mann

Favorite Songs continued

Great is Your Mercy - Donnie McClurkin
I Call You Faithful - Donnie McClurkin

I Give Myself Away - William McDowell

It's Working - Bishop William Murphy
Everlasting God - Bishop William Murphy

The Blood - Smokie Norful

Total Praise - Richard Smallwood

Every Praise - Hezekiah Walker
God Favored Me - Hezekiah Walker
Grateful - Hezekiah Walker

He Promised Me - BeBe Winans

NOTES

Preface: He Knows My Name
1   Stanley, Charles F., *The Charles F. Stanley Life Principles Bible (NKJ)*, "God's Desire to Communicate with Us," (Thomas Nelson, Inc., 2005), page 716.

Introduction: Blessing and Burden
1   Stanley, Charles F., "How God Gets Our Attention" (In Touch Ministries, March 2004), page 7.
2   "Dare to Dream," (The Word for You Today, November 19, 2018), page 46.

Section One
1   "Make Things Right with God," (The Word for You Today, June 13, 2021), page 11.
2   Stanley, Charles F., *The Charles F. Stanley Life Principles Bible (NKJ)*, Life Lessons - Romans 10:17, (Thomas Nelson, Inc., 2005), page 1323.

Chapter 2: Joy in My Dance
1   Triple Negative Breast Cancer Foundation, "What is Triple Negative Breast Cancer," (https://tnbcfoundation.org/what-is-tnbc).
2   Stanley, Charles F., *The Charles F. Stanley Life Principles Bible (NKJ)*: "God's Limitations on Adversity," (Thomas Nelson, Inc., 2005), page 517.

Chapter 3: Somebody's Gotta Have Some Sense
1   "What is Neulasta and how is it used?," RxList (https://www.rxlist.com/neulasta-drug.htm), 2021.

Section Two
Chapter 4: Model for Jesus
1   Article: Bollinger, Ty, "Understanding the 4 Stages of Cancer," (https://thetruthaboutcancer.com/understanding-four-stages-cancer/), February 22, 2020.
2   Stanley, Charles F., *The Charles F. Stanley Life Principles Bible (NKJ)*, "God's Desire to Communicate with Us," (Thomas Nelson, Inc., 2005), page 716.

Section Three
Chapter 7: Count It All Joy

1   Stanley, Charles F., *The Charles F. Stanley Life Principles Bible (NKJ)*, Life Lessons - James 1:2-3, (Thomas Nelson, Inc., 2005), page 1458.

2   Mayo Clinic, "Low blood cell counts: Side effect of cancer treatment," (https://www.mayoclinic.org/diseases-conditions/cancer/in-depth/cancer-treatment/art-20046192).

3   Ibid.

Chapter 8: Inner Voice

1   Tiegreen, Chris., *The One Year Walk with God Devotional*, "Promised Safety," (Tyndale House Publishers, Inc., 2004), page 320.

Section Four

1   Stanley, Charles F., *The Charles F. Stanley Life Principles Bible (NKJ)*, Life Lessons - 2 Corinthians 7:1, (Thomas Nelson, Inc., 2005), page 1356.

Chapter 11: Comforted by His Peace

1   National Breast Cancer Foundation, Inc., "What Is Radiation Therapy and How Does It Work? (https://www.nationalbreastcancer.org/breast-cancer-radiation-therapy).

Chapter 12: My Faith File

1   Stanley, Charles F., *The Charles F. Stanley Life Principles Bible (NKJ)*, "God's Limitations on Adversity," (Thomas Nelson, Inc., 2005), page 823.

Section Five
Chapter 14: In the Morning

1   "How to Win Life's Battles," (The Word for You Today, December 17-22, 2019). "How to Win Life's Battles" is authored by Bob and Debby Gass and published under license from Celebration Enterprises, Inc. Copyright © 2019.

2   Ibid.

3   "What does it mean that we are more than conquerors (Romans 8:37)?" (GotQuestions.org: https://www.gotquestions.org/more-than-conquerors.html)

4   "How to Win Life's Battles," (The Word for You Today, December 17-22, 2019). "How to Win Life's Battles" is authored by Bob

and Debby Gass and published under license from Celebration Enterprises, Inc. Copyright © 2019.

5   Tiegreen, Chris., *The One Year Walk with God Devotional,* "Where You Are," (Tyndale House Publishers, Inc., 2004), page 341.

6   Stanley, Charles F., "Cling to God's Promises," (In Touch Ministries), 2019.

7   "How to Win Life's Battles," (The Word for You Today, December 17-22, 2019. "How to Win Life's Battles" is authored by Bob and Debby Gass and published under license from Celebration Enterprises, Inc. Copyright © 2019.

8   Ibid.

9   Ibid

10 Tiegreen, Chris., *The One Year Walk with God Devotional,* "Where You Are," (Tyndale House Publishers, Inc., 2004), page 341.

11 "How to Win Life's Battles," (The Word for You Today, December 17-22, 2019. "How to Win Life's Battles" is authored by Bob and Debby Gass and published under license from Celebration Enterprises, Inc. Copyright © 2019.

Chapter 15: Blessed to be Used by God

1   Cole, Steven J., "*The People God Uses* (Lesson 89)," Bible.org.

2   Ibid.

3   Ibid.

4   Ibid.

5   "Positioned to Be Blessed," Inspirational and Motivational Sermon, (https://www.youtube.com/results?search_query=Positioned+to+Be+Blessed), 2021.

Epilogue: He Will Never

1   Stanley, Charles F., *The Charles F. Stanley Life Principles Bible (NKJ),* "Life Lessons - Psalm 9:10," (Thomas Nelson, Inc., 2005), page 629.

Acknowledgements

1   Stanley, Charles F., *The Charles F. Stanley Life Principles Bible (NKJ),* Life Lessons - Ecclesiastes 4:9-10, (Thomas Nelson, Inc., 2005), page 761.

GLOSSARY

Carboplatin used in chemotherapy, is an anticancer drug ("antineoplastic" or "cytotoxic") classified as an "alkylating agent. It works in different ways to stop the growth of tumor cells, either by killing the cells, stopping them from dividing, or stopping them from spreading.

Chemotherapy Induced Peripheral Neuropathy (CIPN) - Some of the chemotherapy and other drugs used to treat cancer can damage peripheral nerves. CIPN can cause severe pain and can affect your ability to do things like walk, write, button your shirt, or pick up coins. CIPN can last for weeks, months, or even years after treatment is done. If it gets very bad, it can cause more severe problems like changes in your heart rate and blood pressure, dangerous falls, trouble breathing, paralysis, or organ failure.

Complete blood count (CBC) is a *test* that counts the cells that make up your blood: red blood cells, white blood cells, and platelets. A complete blood count (CBC) is used to evaluate your overall health and detect a wide range of disorders, including anemia, infection, and leukemia.

Computerized Tomography (CT) scan combines a series of X-ray images taken from different angles around your body and uses computer processing to create cross-sectional images (slices) of the bones, blood vessels, and soft tissues inside your body. CT scan images provide more detailed information than plain X-rays do.

DIEP Flap Breast Reconstruction is similar to a muscle-sparing free TRAM flap, except that **no** muscle is used to rebuild the breast. (A muscle-sparing free TRAM flap uses a small amount of muscle.) A DIEP flap is considered a muscle-sparing type of flap. DIEP stands for the deep inferior epigastric perforator artery, which runs through the abdomen.

In a DIEP flap, fat, skin, and blood vessels are cut from the wall of the lower belly and moved up to your chest to rebuild your breast. (In a properly performed DIEP, no muscle is cut or removed; if you're having a DIEP flap, make sure this will be the case.) Your surgeon carefully reattaches the blood vessels of the flap to blood vessels in your chest using microsurgery. Because no muscle is used, most women recover more quickly and have a lower risk of losing abdominal muscle strength with a DIEP flap compared to any of the TRAM flap procedures.

Docetaxel is a toxoid antineoplastic agent used to treat various cancers such as locally advanced or metastatic breast cancer, metastatic prostate cancer, gastric adenocarcinoma, and head and neck cancer. Because the active ingredient, docetaxel, is a strong chemotherapy drug, it also has a long list of side effects. Most of them are typical for drugs in this class, such as nausea, vomiting, and temporary alopecia (hair loss).

Leukopenia is a reduction in the number of white cells in the blood, typical of various diseases.
Different types of cancer, including leukemia, can lead to leukopenia. Cancer treatments can also cause leukopenia, including chemotherapy and radiation therapy (especially when used on large bones, such as those in your legs and pelvis).

Linear Accelerator (LINAC) is the device most commonly used for external beam radiation treatments for patients with cancer. It delivers high-energy x-rays or electrons to the region of the patient's tumor. These treatments can be designed in such a way that they destroy the cancer cells while sparing the surrounding normal tissue. It features several built-in safety measures to ensure that it will deliver the dose as prescribed and is routinely checked by a medical physicist to ensure it is working properly.

Mold Room provides a clinical and technical service for patients who need a course of radiotherapy treatment to the head and neck and, in some cases, the chest area and limbs. These devices are primarily designed to immobilize the area during treatment so that the radiotherapy can be delivered.

Platelets help your blood to clot. A low platelet count (thrombocytopenia) means your body can't stop itself from bleeding. It is a small colorless disk-shaped cell fragment without a nucleus, found in large numbers in blood and involved in clotting.

Red blood cells carry oxygen throughout your body. Your red blood cells' ability to carry oxygen is measured by the amount of hemoglobin in your blood. If your hemoglobin level is low, you're anemic, and your body works much harder to supply oxygen to your tissues. This can make you feel fatigued and short of breath.

Simulator is a diagnostic test that uses radiation waves, called x-rays, to take pictures of your body tissues.

Thrombocytopenia is a condition in which you have a low blood platelet count. Platelets (thrombocytes) are colorless blood cells that help blood clot. Platelets stop bleeding by clumping and forming plugs in blood vessel injuries.

If you have thrombocytopenia, you don't have enough platelets in your blood. Platelets help your blood clot, which stops bleeding. For most people, it's not a big problem. But if you have a severe form, you can bleed spontaneously in your eyes, gums, or bladder or bleed too much when you're injured.

White blood cells help the body's immune system fight infection and other diseases. It's a type of blood cell made in the bone marrow and found in the blood and lymph tissue. A low white blood cell count (leukopenia) leaves your body more open to infection. If an infection develops, your body may be unable to fight it off.

ACKNOWLEDGEMENTS

Gratitude

Two are better than one,
Because they have a good reward for their labor.
For if they fall, one will lift up his companion.
But woe to him who is alone when he falls,
For he has no one to help him up.

~ *Ecclesiastes 4:9-10* ~

I am forever grateful to each of you for allowing God to use you during my dance! As Charles Stanley says, "God never calls on any of His children to 'go it alone' in their walk with Him. We need each other, not only to receive help and encouragement, but to give it as well."[1]

To my pastor, Bishop Michael F. Jones — shepherd of Friendly Temple Missionary Baptist Church in St. Louis, I am so thankful for your prayers, preaching, and teaching of God's Word, and for your words of support and encouragement throughout my dance!

Many thanks to my dad, Jasper Powell, who wanted to be by my side. Your numerous calls to check on me was comforting!

To my *Aunt Catherine Vick Battle, thank you for traveling with my mom, for being supportive, and for your prayers!

To my aunts, Bobbie J. Powell and Shirley Singleton — both breast cancer survivors, thank you for your willingness to share your experience, answer my many questions, and your support!

Raymond F. Allen, Jr., what a trooper! Thank God for transportation. Throughout my dance, you drove and flew to see me. Many thanks for the roses the day after each chemo treatment and for your support. You have always been a blessing to me!

Cousin Mattie Robinson, a prayer warrior. Thank you for bending your knees with my mom to praise the Lord for my healing!

Jean Dae, thank you for allowing the Lord to use you to connect me to the individuals who would administer the care that was appropriate for me!

To my lifelong friend, Thomas Wayne Headd, Jr., thank you for our talks, your spiritual counsel, prayers, and teachable moments!

Before the arrival of my mom, First Lady Cynthia Williams — my sister in Christ and sorority sister — who without hesitation, accompanied me to the doctor's office to discuss the next steps with my physician. A nurse, her knowledge and understanding of the concepts and processes was a tremendous blessing. To her husband, Reverend, Dr. Jeffrey Williams, my dear friend and brother in Christ, and the congregation of New Christian Fellowship, thank you for your prayers and for being a financial blessing!

God knows what He's doing. He places the right people in your life to do His Will. Former First Lady Vickie Calmese, one of God's foot soldiers, a woman of service, is the person God blessed me with. My sister in Christ accompanied me to doctor visits, was present at all chemo sessions, and stayed with me through tests and surgery. She, a retired nurse, made sure I understood the spiritual and medical process. When I would thank her for being with me, she would thank me for allowing her to witness the dance!

Many thanks to my Bible study group that is under the umbrella of the Biblical Business Training (BBT) family: Kim Davidson, Karen McMurray, Carol Mayfield Fletcher, and LaTonya Alexander for our weekly Bible study sessions, your prayers, support, and encouragement during what could have been a very challenging time. You are truly a gift from God!

A very special thank you to Joyce Scott, who stood in the gap for my mom, who could not be with me during my surgery because of an injury that left her temporarily semi-immobile. Joyce, who was to only drop me off at the hospital the morning of the surgery where friends were meeting me, took her fill-in momma duties seriously and stayed until I was out of surgery and resting comfortably in the hospital room!

Zanetta Harris, your sincere willingness to donate your hair, so that I too could have hair, left me speechless. Praise the Lord! Little did my mom know, her rubbing of my head as an infant would prepare me for such a moment as this. I grew up with a perfectly shaped head that allowed me to rock a bald look. Thank you for the love and support and the frequent check-ups and check-ins!

Many thanks to the ladies of the Breakfast Club, a local nonprofit breast cancer support group, for sharing your stories, support, and for the educational sessions. A very special thanks to Mrs. Ella Jones for her endless support and encouragement and to Jan Whitlock, we met as new members at a Breakfast Club meeting. Thank you for your continued friendship!

Many thanks to Real Men Wear Pink — STL, a nonprofit organization, for their fundraising efforts to provide support for women with breast cancer! And a very special thank you to Sonya and Maurice Burns for nominating me to be one of the recipients of those funds!

Many thanks to the women of the Empowerment Zone: Gail Taylor, Paula Hughes Southerland, Karen McMurray, Linda Tate, Denise Williams, Tracy Blue, Ralonda Jasper, Zundra Bryant, Darcella Craven, and Joyce Wade for the care package and your generosity!

Many thanks to Curtis Scroggins, my accountability partner, for encouraging me and keeping me on task to give my testimony! And a very special thanks to Kim Fletcher who encouraged me to write the book and not focus so much on the how and who of publishing the book… "Finish the manuscript," she would often say!

There are so many family members and friends to thank. You have all been such a blessing and have touched my life throughout this dance. Thank you all for the acts of kindness, prayers, calls, visits, cards, support, and monetary assistance. Names are in no particular order: Ann Meyers, Adrian Bracy, Gilda Brewton, JoSezettea Keeton, Robert Powell, James Vick, Louis Battle, Jr., Jacqueline Boleware-Faniel, Angela Battle, Honeya Boleware, *Dyane Wilson, *Valerie Bryant, Deirdre Singleton, Cyndi Knight, *Jasper Powell, Jr., Doris Gross, Cheryl Burton, Renee Thomas-Woods, Hank McGee, Vivian Dunn, Doreen Carmichael, Joann York, Connie Hill-Johnson, Lillie Williams, Arnita Jones, Robin Anderson, *Jackie Olden, Annetta Canady, Lisa Cooksey-Cannon, Nichelle Womack, Marlynn Chambers, Siiyna Williams, Joshua Carrawell, Corneilus Bowe, Pierre Smith, Lynette Sledge-Watson, Rinoldo and Michelle Allen, Valerie Raise, Marqela Goff, Juanita Roy, Erika Harris, Deborah Hamilton, *Louise Morrison, Gerome Cummins, Ernestine Daniel, Adrienne Thomas, Hank McGee, Cynthia Scroggins, Amber Simpson, Michael Pattin, Rob and Lauren Bergtholdt, Dee Buhlig, Sandy Simmons, Jeff and Leah Cross, Elaine Young, doctors and staff of Barnes Jewish Christian Hospital and Siteman Cancer Center, and the Gateway to Hope team!

A very special thank you to Raymond F. Allen, Jr., Carol Boulden, Gilda Brewton, Betty Brooks, Thomas W. Headd, Jr., Sheryl Hudson, Pam Love, Karen McMurray, Curtis Scroggins, Cynthia Scroggins, Rev. Dr. Jeffrey Williams, and Dr. Mary Willoughby for taking time to review this book and provide invaluable feedback.

If I have omitted anyone, please blame my head and not my heart!

Thank God for His faithfulness!

*Deceased

Spread the Word

Victoriously Dancing Through Life, Orchestrated by God

Thank you for reading *Victoriously Dancing Through Life, Orchestrated by God*. It is my hope and prayer that you have been immeasurably blessed and empowered by God through my story. Please share it with your friends and family and mention it on your social media sites so someone dealing with cancer can be blessed by it. I also welcome hearing from you. Let me know how *Victoriously Dancing Through Life* has helped you to get through your "it." You can reach me on my Facebook group page, Battle Beautifully.

Blessings,
Jacquie

Final Thoughts...

Final Thoughts...

_____
_____
_____
_____
_____
_____
_____
_____
_____
_____
_____
_____
_____
_____
_____
_____
_____
_____
_____
_____
_____
_____
_____
_____
_____
_____
_____
_____
_____
_____

Final Thoughts...